Legal Aspects of Consent

Other books in the **Legal Aspects of Health Care** series:

Legal Aspects of Patient Confidentiality by Bridgit Dimond
Legal Aspects of Pain Management by Bridgit Dimond

Also by the same author published by Quay Books, a division of Mark Allen Publishing Limited:

Patients' Rights, Responsibilities and the Nurse, second edition
Mental Health (Patients in the Community) Act 1995: An introductory guide

Legal Aspects of Consent

BJN monograph

Legal Aspects of Health Care series

Bridgit Dimond

Quay Books

Mark Allen Publishing Ltd

Quay Books Division, Mark Allen Publishing Limited,
Jesses Farm, Snow Hill, Dinton, Wiltshire, SP3 5HN

British Library Cataloguing-in-Publication Data
A catalogue record is available for this book

© Bridgit Dimond 2003
ISBN 1 85642 217 8

Printed in the UK by Cromwell Press, Trowbridge, Wiltshire

Contents

Foreword

We lawyers are unpopular people and that is not surprising. We come along after the event and tell people what they should have done (or not done). This is particularly annoying for conscientious professionals who have to take sensitive and difficult decisions — about what to tell a patient, whether the patient is able to agree to or refuse treatment, whether he or she has in fact done so — in the heat of the moment. Much better if they have a clear idea of the legal principles and sensible guidance about how to apply them in advance. That is what Bridgit Dimond has set out to give you in this book.

But it goes further than that. The health care professions, the Department of Health and the NHS service providers are developing models of 'good professional practice' in this area. If there is clear professional guidance about what is good practice on a particular point, then a professional may have to justify departing from it in an individual case. It is harder to say that it was regarded as acceptable by a 'responsible body of medical opinion' (in the well known test laid down in *Bolam* v. *Friern Hospital Management Committee* [1957]). So the responsible professional needs to know what the guidance says as well as what the law says.

And on top of all that is the Human Rights Act 1998. The very essence of the European Convention on Human Rights is respect for human dignity and human freedom, as the European Court of Human Rights said in the case of Diane Pretty (the motor neurone disease sufferer who wanted her husband to be allowed to help her to commit suicide). The court also said that the notion of personal autonomy is an important principle underlying the right to respect for private life in Article 8. This does not mean that the patient's wishes always prevail.

But you need a book like this to tell you when they do and when they don't.

Brenda Hale
December 2002

Preface

Like the first book in this series, the law relating to patient confidentiality, this monograph follows the publication of a series of articles in the *British Journal of Nursing* on consent. The advantages of a book for health professionals setting out the law and practice on consent led to Quay Books agreeing that the articles, updated and revised, could form the basis of a concise publication covering the main concerns which arise in respecting the law relating to consent.

Like the other books in this series, this is intended for all health professionals, health service managers and patient groups and their representatives. It aims to use a style which avoids legal jargon and by the use of illustrating situations or cases provides an easy guide to the law relating to consent. Since by far the majority of health professionals are women, she rather than he and her rather than his has been used for the registered practitioners whose role is considered in the following pages.

Many readers may not be acquainted with basic facts of the legal system and so these are briefly set out in the first chapter. It is hoped that this book, like the others in this series, will provide a succinct, useful basis from which practitioners and others can extend their knowledge of the law for the protection of their patients, their colleagues and themselves.

Bridgit Dimond
October 2002

Acknowledgements

I should like to thank all those many practitioners with whom I have come into contact through conferences and teaching who have raised with me the questions and issues which form the basis of this book. I am also indebted to the efficient and cheerful support of my editor Binkie Mais. As always, I am grateful to the constant support and encouragement of Bette Griffiths, who once again prepared the index and tables of cases and statutes.

Finally, I would like to acknowledge the advice, assistance and encouragement of Tessa Shellens over many years and, it is to Tessa that this book is dedicated.

1

Sources of law and guidance

Introduction

This first chapter sets out the legal basis from which our laws of consent derive and it also explains the provisions of the Human Rights Act 1998 and the legal system of the UK. The information is of necessity brief and readers may be interested in reading more detailed works set out in further reading on *page 225*.

Source of law

Our laws derive from two principal sources: Acts of Parliament/ statutory instruments (known as a statute or legislation) and decided cases. (See the *Glossary* for further explanations of legal terms.)

Legislation

Legislation, as well as consisting of Acts of Parliament (approval by the Houses of Commons and Lords and the Queen's assent) would include directives and regulations emanating from the European Community, which we as a member state are required to implement and obey (see below).

Legislation can be primary or secondary. As primary legislation it consists of Acts of Parliament, known as statutes, which come into force at a date set either in the initial Act of Parliament or a date subsequently fixed by order of a Minister (ie. by statutory instrument). The date of enforcement is often later than the date it is passed by the two Houses of Parliament and signed by the Crown. The statute sometimes gives power to a Minister to enact more detailed laws and these regulations are known as secondary legislation. Statutory instruments which are quoted in the text are an example of this secondary legislation.

Common law, judge-made law, case law

The other main source of law is the decisions of the courts. This source is known as case law, or judge-made law or the common law. The courts form a hierarchy and the highest court in this country is the House of Lords. The courts lay down principles which must be followed by courts below that level, unless the decision can be distinguished on the basis that it is not relevant to the case before it. If the House of Lords sets down a specific principle, known as a precedent, then this is binding on all courts in the country, except itself (ie. the House of Lords does not have to follow its own precedents).

In the case of Diane Pretty (*R. (on the application of Pretty)* v. *DPP* [2001]), the House of Lords decided that her application (that her husband should be given an advanced immunity against any possible proceedings under the Suicide Act 1961 if he were to aid and abet her suicide) could not be granted. They did not find that her human rights as set out in the European Convention on Human Rights (see below) were breached by the Suicide Act 1961. (The case is discussed further in *Chapter 19*.)

The decisions of the courts are reported so that lawyers and judges can refer to a specific case and the principles established by it. These principles are known as the *ratio decidendi* and can be applied to any matters in dispute. Judges might also make statements about wider matters not directly necessary to the decision in the case before them, and these statements are known as *obiter dicta*. These may be of persuasive authority and interest in subsequent cases but they are not binding as precedents. If there is a dispute between a case and a statute the latter would take priority: judges have to follow an Act of Parliament. Thus, in the Diane Pretty case which is considered in *Chapter 19*, had the House of Lords thought that the Suicide Act 1961 was contrary to the European Convention on Human Rights (see below), then it could have referred this statute back to Parliament for review. (In practice the House of Lords did not consider that there was any clash between the Suicide Act 1961 and the articles in the European Convention on Human Rights.) Parliament can enact legislation which would overrule a principle established in the courts.

Human Rights Act 1998

This came into force in England, Wales and Northern Ireland on 2 October 2000 and on Devolution in Scotland. It incorporates the articles of the European Convention on Human Rights (contained in Schedule 1 to the Act) into our laws. (Schedule 1 can be found in the *Appendix* to this book.) The Act:

- requires all public authorities to implement the articles of the European Convention on Human Rights
- gives a right to anyone who alleges that a public authority has failed to respect those rights to bring an action in the courts of this country
- enables judges who consider that legislation is incompatible with the Articles of the Convention to refer that legislation back to Parliament.

While there are no specific articles which expressly consider the law on consent, Article 2 on the right to life, Article 3 on the right not to be subjected to torture or to inhuman or degrading treatment or punishment, Article 5 on the right to liberty and security of person and Article 8 on the right to respect for private and family life and correspondence all relate to some of the issues which arise in the laws on consent and will be considered in subsequent chapters.

In the case concerning Siamese twins, the Court of Appeal had to decide if it was lawful to allow an operation to proceed which would automatically lead to the death of the one child who was dependent upon her sister's heart and lungs for survival. There was evidence that the dependent child Mary was killing her sister Jodie. While both children had a right to life under Article 2 of the European Convention on Human Rights, the Court of Appeal held that the best interests of the twin who had the heart and lungs should prevail over the other and that the operation should go ahead (in *Re A. (minors)* 2000).

Effect of the European Community

Since the United Kingdom signed the Treaty of Rome in 1972, the UK has become one of the member states of the European Community. The effect of this is that the UK is now subject to the laws made by the Council of Ministers and the European Commission. In addition, secondary legislation of the European Community in the form of regulations is binding on the member states. Directives of the Community must be incorporated by Act of Parliament into the law of each member state. Appeals from UK courts on EC laws can be made to the European Court of Justice in Luxembourg which gives interpretations of the European laws. Their decisions are binding on the courts of member states.

Criminal and civil law

Issues relating to consent arise in both the criminal laws and civil laws. Criminal offences which may be defined by both statutes and the common law can be prosecuted in the criminal courts of this country. A public prosecution is brought in the name of the Crown and the prosecution have to establish that the offence has been committed beyond reasonable doubt. (It is also possible to bring a private prosecution, but this can be costly and it is often difficult to secure a conviction.) The offence of assault is a criminal offence under the Offences Against the Person Act 1861, battery is an offence at common law. An absence of consent to treatment could therefore lead to criminal prosecution against the perpetrator. If an operation which is totally contrary to reasonable professional practice even with the consent of the patient, this consent may not be sufficient to defend the surgeon against criminal proceedings for causing grievous bodily harm. (See *Chapter 22* on consent to the amputation of healthy limbs.)

In addition, the same acts could constitute a civil wrong and be actionable by the victim in the civil courts. The civil courts can award compensation and can issue other orders such as an order for specific performance, an injunction, or a declaration. The claimant must establish his or her case on a balance of probabilities, which, in contrast to the standard of proof in the criminal courts is a lighter burden.

Law and ethics

There is considerable overlap between the law and ethics. One's ethics or moral standards derive from a variety of sources; religion, upbringing, personal experience all lead to a person's ethical values. In any democratic society one would hope that there would be a strong reciprocal relationship between the law and ethics. Therefore, many civil and criminal wrongs would also be regarded as ethically wrong. However, there may be ethical views which are not part of the law. In this book we are concerned with the law and there can be little discussion of ethical issues. In many of the situations we discuss there is also a moral or ethical perspective and the reader is referred to the reading list for sources on ethics in health care for further discussion.

Department of Health guidance

The Department of Health (DoH) has published a *Reference Guide to Consent for Examination or Treatment* (DoH, 2001a). This is a comprehensive document covering a wide range of situations. The appendices include the principles to be followed in applications to court when there is doubt as to the patient's capacity to consent, as well as further reading and legal references. Forms which can be used as evidence that consent has been given have been published and were implemented from April 2002 (DoH, 2001b).

The Department of Health has also provided, as part of the reference guide, additional guides for relatives and carers, parents, adults, children and young people and people with learning difficulties (with helpful pictures). It also provides a single sheet entitled '12 key points on consent: the law in England' which could be put on the notice boards of wards or departmental offices in England. All those involved in obtaining consent should ensure that they have easy access to this information and that it is updated at regular intervals. It is the Department of Health's intention that the reference guide should be revised on a regular basis. It can be accessed via the Department of Health's website (DoH, 2002c).

Kennedy report

An inquiry was set up to investigate the circumstances leading to the deaths of several children who underwent cardiac surgery in Bristol and was chaired by Professor Kennedy. His report was published in 2001 (Kennedy, 2001) and made extensive and radical recommendations for reform within the NHS. The recommendations will be referred to in several chapters in this book.

Professional advice

Many of the registered practitioners who are involved in consent issues with their patients, have guidance from their professional bodies on the law and professional practice relating to consent to treatment. For example, the Nursing and Midwifery Council (NMC) (NMC, 2002) in Clause 3 of its *Code of professional conduct* states, 'As a registered nurse or midwife, you must obtain consent before you give any treatment or care'. This statement is then further explained in sub-clauses 3.1–3.11. The General Medical Council (GMC, 2000) has also issued guidance on consent for its registered medical practitioners. Failure to comply with the codes of professional practice and other guidance issued by a registration body could result in a practitioner facing professional conduct proceedings with the ultimate threat of being struck off from the register.

Employment law

Most health professionals are employees who have a contract of employment with their employers. This contract may spell out explicitly duties in relation to the care of the patient, the observation of a duty of confidentiality and duties in relation to health and safety. In addition, the law implies certain terms into the contract of employment. For example, under these implied terms an employee would be expected to obey the reasonable orders of the employer, to act with reasonable care and skill and to recognise the duty of confidentiality. There is an implied duty that an employer will take reasonable care of the health and safety at work of the employee. Failure to obey express or implied terms could result in an employee facing disciplinary action, with the ultimate sanction of dismissal from her post. Following a dismissal, an employee with the requisite length of service could apply to an employment tribunal for a declaration that the dismissal was unfair and for compensation and/or reinstatement.

Any employee who failed to follow the legal principles relating to consent to treatment could face criminal, civil, professional conduct and disciplinary proceedings.

References

Dimond B (2001) *Legal Aspects of Nursing.* 3rd edn. Pearson Education, London

Department of Health (2001a) *Reference Guide to Consent for Examination or Treatment.* DoH, London

Department of Health (2001b) *Good Practice in Consent Implementation Guide: Consent to Examination and Treatment.* DoH, London

Department of Health (2002c) online at: http://www.doh.gov.uk

General Medical Council (2000) *Seeking Patients' Consent: The ethical considerations.* GMC, London

Kennedy I (2001) Bristol Royal Infirmary Inquiry Learning from Bristol: the report of the public inquiry into children's heart surgery at the Bristol Royal Infirmary 1984–1995. Command paper CM 5207. Stationery Office, London

Re A. (minors) (conjoined twins: surgical separation) The Times Law Report 10 October 2000; [2001] Fam 147 CA

Nursing and Midwifery Council (2002) *Code of professional conduct 2002.* NMC, London

R. (on the application of Pretty) v. *DPP* [2001] UKHL 61, [2001] 3 WLR 1598

2

The mentally competent adult

Box 2.1: Case scenario

Following a road accident, Ralph, a twenty-five-year-old man, has been told that his hand has been so badly injured that it cannot be saved and he needs to have it amputated. He says that he would prefer to die than have an artificial 'hook'. The ward sister arranges for him to be visited by a young woman who has had a similar amputation following injury and has learnt to use a prosthesis. Ralph still refuses. He is visited by a psychologist who considers that he has the necessary mental capacity to make his own decisions. His family and girlfriend plead with the surgeons to carry on regardless of his refusal, since he is too young and immature to understand the implications of his decision. He repeats to the nursing staff that he knows he will probably die without surgery, but he has made up his mind.

Introduction

Before treatment commences, the law requires that the health professional obtains the consent of a mentally competent person. Simple though this principle seems, many additional questions and problems arise, eg. what if a person lacks mental competence? What about children? What about the way in which consent should be given? And, what about rights of relatives? This chapter examines the principle relating to the right of refusal by a mentally competent adult.

Without the consent of a mentally competent adult, any

treatment or care which involves touching the person could be considered a trespass to the person. The fact that consent has been given is the most important defence in facing any such action. The burden is upon the claimant (ie. the person bringing any claim — used to be known as the plaintiff) to prove that a valid consent was not given.

Trespass to the person

An action for trespass (which belongs to a group of civil wrongs known as 'torts') is one of the oldest remedies in law (known as a right of action in law); it includes an assault and a battery. An action for assault arises where the employee of the defendant (in this context it is normally the employer of the health professional who would be sued because of its vicarious liability for the actions of the employee) causes a claimant reasonable apprehension of the infliction of a battery upon him/her; a battery arises where there is intentional and direct application of force to another person.

Assault and battery are also used to describe possible criminal actions, but when we are using the terms in relation to a trespass to the person, we are referring to a civil action brought in the civil courts (ie. County Court, High Court) for compensation by a claimant.

Unlike an action for negligence, harm does not have to be proved. The mere fact that a trespass has occurred is sufficient to bring an action. The action is known as actionable *per se*, ie. actionable without proof of harm having been suffered. Trespass can also exist in relation to land and to goods. The mere touching of another person's property or possessions can constitute in law an actionable trespass. Clearly, however, an exception to trespass exists for the ordinary social contact of everyday life. For example, a person could not enter the tube at rush hour and say: 'Don't touch me or I'll sue for trespass to the person.' However, any deliberate touching of another person may constitute an assault or battery (*Box 2.2*). An action can still constitute a trespass even when it is performed in the best interests of a person who is mentally capable but has not given consent.

> ### Box 2.2: The case of *Re F. (a mental patient: sterilisation)* [1990]
>
> In this case, Lord Goff said:
>
> > *A prank that gets out of hand, an over-friendly slap on the back, these things may transcend the bounds of lawfulness, without being characterised as hostile... Any touching of another's body is, in the absence of lawful excuse, capable of amounting to a battery and a trespass. Furthermore, in the case of medical treatment, we have to bear well in mind the libertarian principle of self-determination, which, to adopt the words of Cardozo J (an American judge), recognises that:*
> >
> > > *Every human being of adult years and sound mind has a right to determine what shall be done with his own body; and a surgeon who performs an operation without his patient's consent commits an assault for which he is liable in damages. (Schloendorff v. Society of New York Hospital 211 NY 125 (1914)*

In the case scenario (*Box 2.1*), Ralph appears to be mentally capable. He has even been visited by a psychologist who has declared that he is mentally competent for the purposes of making the decision about whether or not to have his hand amputated. (The determination of competence is considered in *Chapter 6*.) He is over eighteen years and therefore an adult. Ralph is entitled to refuse to give consent for a good reason, a bad reason or no reason at all (*Re MB. (adult medical treatment)* [1997], see *Chapter 12*). There can be no question of overruling his refusal. His right of autonomy permits him to make such decisions, even if death is the likely outcome.

Operating without consent

Let us imagine the following outcome. Ralph's family and girlfriend know that Ralph is a health fanatic and is in training for a place in the national gymnastics team. They consider that because of the trauma of the accident, he is, at this point, incapable of accepting such a reversal to his lifestyle and to his future ambitions and, in the short term, cannot cope with the situation. They discuss the situation with the ward staff and surgeons and ask that the operation should go ahead because they know that once it is performed Ralph will accept the situation and then learn to adapt to a new way of life and adopt new interests and hobbies. They suggest that the doctors should take Ralph down for surgery, telling him that only conservative action would be taken. In other words, his refusal should be overruled. They point out that had the amputation taken place when Ralph was brought into the hospital unconscious, he would have been faced with a *fait accompli*. They say that they are prepared to sign any consent form for the operation on Ralph.

On the basis of this agreement, Ralph is taken to theatre. He does not sign any form. He understands that he is being operated on for his hand to be saved if possible and no amputation is to take place. When he returns from theatre, he is told that the operation has taken place and that unfortunately his hand could not be saved and an amputation has taken place. He is extremely upset. Instead of accepting the situation and learning to adjust to it, he wishes to take legal action against those who carried out the surgery without his consent and he brings an action for trespass to the person. The lawyers to the trust suggest that the action should be defended as the doctors at all times acted in the best interests of Ralph. The outcome is likely to be a successful action for Ralph.

Table 2.1: Reasons why Ralph would be successful in any court action if his hand was amputated without his consent

- He did not give consent to the operation and therefore the operation constituted a trespass to his person.

- He had the mental capacity to know what was being intended, to retain the information and make a decision upon it. He knew the likely consequence of his refusal and was mentally competent to make the decision.

- The fact that he has not suffered harm, but in fact has benefited from the operation, is irrelevant to the fact that it was a trespass to the person.

- The fact that the relatives gave consent is irrelevant. In law relatives do not have the power to give consent to treatment on behalf of patients who are over eighteen years old, even if the patients lack the mental capacity to make their own decisions and here, of course, Ralph has the requisite mental capacity.

Valid consent X

To be valid, consent must be given by a person who has the necessary mental capacity. This could include a child of sixteen or seventeen who has a statutory right to give consent, or a child under sixteen years who has a right recognised at common law (ie. judge-made law) to give consent, provided the child is 'Gillick competent' (*Chapters 8 and 9*). Consent must be given voluntarily — there must be no coercion, deceit or fraud.

Sufficient information must be given to the person so that he/she understands the basics of what is proposed. There are advantages in ensuring that the consent is evidenced in writing, but the writing is not the consent, the consent is the actual agreement by the person that what is proposed can go ahead. Consent can be given in general terms to a particular procedure, without every single aspect being explained to the patient, but failure to warn of the significant risks of substantial harm could constitute an action for breach of the duty of care to inform (this will be considered in *Chapters 4* and *5*).

Ms B. case

In the recent case of *Re B.* [2002], the President of the Family Division stated that a mentally competent patient could ask for her ventilator to be switched off and that it was a trespass to her person to treat her without her consent. The facts are shown in *Box 2.3*.

Box 2.3: Facts of Re B. [2002]

Ms B. suffered a ruptured blood vessel in her neck which damaged her spinal cord. As a consequence she was paralysed from the neck down and was on a ventilator. She was of sound mind and knew that there was no cure for her condition. She asked for the ventilator to be switched off. Her doctors wished her to try out some special rehabilitation to improve the standard of her care and felt that an intensive care ward was not a suitable location for such a decision to be made. They were reluctant to perform such an action as switching off the ventilator without the court's approval. Ms B. applied to court for a declaration to be made that the ventilator could be switched off.

The main issue in the case was the mental competence of Ms B. If she were held to be mentally competent, then she could refuse to have life saving treatment for a good reason, a bad reason or no reason at all. She was interviewed by two psychiatrists who gave evidence to the court that she was mentally competent. The judge held that she was entitled to refuse to be ventilated. The judge Dame Elizabeth Butler-

Schloss, President of the Family Division held that Ms B. possessed the requisite mental capacity to make decisions regarding her treatment and thus the administration of artificial respiration by the trust against her wishes amounted to an unlawful trespass. It was reported on 29 April 2002 that Ms B. had died peacefully in her sleep after the ventilator had been switched off.

Withdrawal of consent

Just as a mentally competent adult can give a valid consent, so can this consent be withdrawn at any time, unless it has been given under contractual arrangements which limit the withdrawing of consent. Another exception would be where the patient has ceased to be mentally competent and the withdrawal of consent would be contrary to his or her best interests. For example, a mentally competent patient may agree to have a termination of pregnancy which is to be undertaken in two stages, first the taking of medication then admission to hospital for the termination to be clinically supervised. If a woman has taken the medication which is to induce a miscarriage, but then goes on a drinking spree, which means that she is not mentally capable of making her decisions, she would not be able to withdraw her consent to the abortion, firstly because it is already in process, and secondly because she lacks the mental capacity to make an effective withdrawal of the original consent. A case where a husband withdrew consent to the posthumous use of his sperm is considered in *Chapter 24* (*Centre for Reproductive Medicine* v. *U* [2002]).

Guidance on consent to treatment

The Department of Health (2001a) published a reference guide to consent to treatment which it is intended will be regularly updated with changes in statute and case law. It also prepared practical guidance for the NHS with new forms (DoH, 2001b) which were to be used from April 2002 (*Chapter 3*).

The recommendations of the Kennedy report (Kennedy, 2001) on paediatric heart surgery in Bristol also emphasise the importance of respect and honesty being at the centre of the relationship between health professional and patient.

Some of the specific recommendations made in the Kennedy report (Kennedy, 2001) are shown in *Box 2.4*. Other recommendations are set out in *Chapters 4* and *5*.

Box 2.4: Recommendations of the Kennedy report on consent

1. In a patient-centred healthcare service patients must be involved, wherever possible, in decisions about their treatment and care.
5. Information should be tailored to the needs, circumstances and wishes of the individual.
23. We note and endorse the recent statement on consent produced by the Department of Health's *Reference Guide to Consent for Examination or Treatment* (DoH, 2001a). It should inform the practice of all healthcare professionals in the NHS and be introduced into practice in all trusts.
24. The process of informing the patient, and obtaining consent to a course of treatment, should be regarded as a process and not a one-off event consisting of obtaining a patient's signature on a form.
24. The process of consent should apply not only to surgical procedures but also to all clinical procedures and examinations which involve any form of touching. This must not mean more forms: it means more communication.

Jehovah's Witnesses

One of the most frequent examples of patients refusing life-saving treatment is when Jehovah's Witnesses refuse to have a blood transfusion. As mentally competent adults their right to refuse such treatment must be respected and the Royal College of Surgeons drew up a code of practice for the surgical management of Jehovah's Witnesses in 1996. It emphasises that, 'if the patient is able to give an informed and rational opinion or if an applicable advance direction (see *Chapter 16* of this book) exists, then this should be acted upon. If they are not, the clinical judgement of the doctor should take precedence over the opinion of relatives and associates.' In the case of *Re T.* [1992] a pregnant woman signed a form, under the influence of her mother a Jehovah's Witness, that she would not wish to have a blood transfusion, at a time when such treatment seemed extremely unlikely. The Court of Appeal held that there is a rebuttable presumption that adults have the capacity to consent to or refuse treatment and, in this case, this presumption could be rebutted since there was evidence that the patient was under the influence of her mother and a blood transfusion was in the patient's best interests.

Exceptions to the right of self-determination of the mentally competent adult

While the general principle is that a mentally competent adult has the right to give or withhold consent to treatment, there are exceptions as a result of public health legislation. Section 37 of the Public Health (Control of Diseases) Act 1984 enables a justice of the peace, on the application of the local authority, if satisfied that a person is suffering from a notifiable disease and it is necessary in order to prevent the spread of infection, to remove the person to suitable accommodation.

The Public Health (Infectious Diseases) regulations 1988 S. I. 1988 No.1546 enable section 37 to be applied to those suffering from AIDS as though it were a notifiable disease.

In addition, the House of Lords (*R.* v. *Brown* [1993]) has held that consent to sado-masochistic acts is not a valid defence to the criminal charge of inflicting violence upon oneself or others. This case and the amputation of healthy limbs is considered in *Chapter 22*.

There are also statutory powers to compel those persons suffering from mental disorder who are detained under the Mental Health Act 1983 to receive treatment (*Chapter 25*).

Conclusion

Recognising that Ralph has the right to determine his own life and treatment is difficult for relatives and professionals. Only if there is clear evidence that he lacks the mental capacity to make that decision could his refusal be overruled and action taken in his best interests. Paternalistic action cannot be a defence against an action for trespass brought by a mentally competent adult. In the next chapter we will consider the form that any consent should take and when writing is required. However, as emphasised in the Kennedy report, obtaining consent is a process of communication, not simply the signing of a form.

References

Re B. (consent to treatment: capacity) The Times Law Report 26 March 2002, [2002] 2 All ER 449

Centre for Reproductive Medicine v. *U* [2002] EWCA Civ 565, *The Independent* 1 May, 2002 CA

Department of Health (2001a) *Reference Guide to Consent for Examination or Treatment*; online at: http://www.doh.gov.uk/consent

Department of Health (2001b) *Good practice in consent implementation guide*. Department of Health, London

Re F. (a mental patient: sterilisation) [1990] 2 AC 1

Kennedy I (2001) Bristol Royal Infirmary Inquiry. Learning from Bristol: the report of the public inquiry into children's heart surgery at the Bristol Royal Infirmary 1984–1995. Command paper CM 5207. Stationery Office, London

Re MB. (adult medical treatment) [1997] 2 FLR 426

R. v. *Brown* [1993] 2 All ER 75

Royal College of Surgeons (1996) *Code of Practice for the Surgical Management of Jehovah's Witnesses*. RCS, London

Re T. [1992] 4 All ER 649

Schloendorff v. *Society of New York Hospital* 211 NY 125 (1914)

3

The different forms of consent

Box 3.1: Case scenario

Mary, following preoperative medication, was taken to theatre for a biopsy for possible breast cancer. When the theatre staff went through their check list they could not find a consent form. The consultant surgeon said that he had seen her in the outpatients' department two weeks before and she had given a clear consent, not only for the biopsy but also for a radical mastectomy should the results show that to be necessary. He said that he had no problems with continuing the operation. The theatre sister was unsure of the legal position.

Introduction

Consent is the agreement by a mentally competent person, voluntarily and without deceit or fraud, to an action which without that consent would be a trespass to the person. (See *Chapter 2* for discussion of trespass to the person.) Evidence of the fact that consent has been given could be a signed document, the spoken words of the patient or the non-verbal actions of the patient implying consent. All these different forms of showing that consent is being given are equally valid in law but clearly vary considerably in evidential terms.

Consent in writing

This is by far the best form of providing evidence that consent has been given. The document is not the actual consent, but evidence that the patient agreed to the procedure. The Department of Health (2001b) has recommended various forms which can be used to record the fact that consent has been given. They include forms for completion by the adult patient, by a child and parent of a child, and also a form where a person lacks the mental competence to give consent which will be considered in *Chapter 7*. It was recommended that these forms should be used from April 2002. Any health professional can make use of the forms since unlike the earlier forms issued in 1992 they do not just relate to treatment by doctors and dentists. There are considerable advantages in other health professionals such as nurses, midwives, physiotherapists and therapeutic radiographers making use of the forms. There are advantages in obtaining evidence in writing that consent has been given, when the treatment involves any risks or where there could be a subsequent dispute over whether consent was given.

Consent form 1 is the form to be used by mentally competent adults, and many NHS trusts have taken the basic form as suggested by the Department of Health and adapted it for specific types of treatment. The basic outline ensures that all the steps which are required in securing a valid consent are taken. Relatives do not have a right to give consent on behalf of another adult, whether that person is mentally competent or not. Consent form 3 can be used where the patient does not lose consciousness.

What is covered by the written consent

The explanation of the intended treatment should include details of what is actually proposed together with information about the significant risks of substantial harm (see *Chapter 5* for further discussion on this). However, it is not a requirement that every single aspect of the procedures would have to be mentioned to secure a valid consent. What if a patient after surgery discovered that he had been given a pain killer administered by a pessary? Could he maintain that that was a trespass to his person, since he had not given specific consent to administration of medicines in that format? The answer is probably 'No', since provided that he had given consent to the overall treatment to be given, his consent to each and every procedure within that heading would not be required (*Sidaway* v. *Bethlem Royal Hospital Governors* [1985]). If it becomes known that certain types of administration of medicines or other procedures cause disquiet to patients, then there would be justification for ensuring that the patient was aware of these in advance, to prevent subsequent complaints.

Consent by word of mouth

On a day-to-day basis, most health professionals work on consent by word of mouth as the basis for performing regular routine care and treatment. 'Are you ready to have your injection?', if responded to by a clear 'Yes', is an example of consent by word of mouth. It would be a ridiculous requirement of bureaucracy if written consent were required for every item of care or procedure. Normally there would be no problems, but if subsequently the patient stated that consent had not been given to such a procedure, unless another person overheard the patient's agreement, it would be one person's word against another.

Non-verbal consent

Sometimes known as implied consent, this relates to the behaviour of the patient which indicates to the health professional that the patient is agreeing to the proposed treatment. For example, instead of responding by saying 'Yes' to the question 'Are you ready to have your injection?', the patient might nod his/her head in agreement. No word is spoken by the patient. There is no consent by word of mouth, but the nodding conveys to the nurse that the patient is agreeing to the injection. The nurse could, therefore, proceed to give the patient the injection, knowing that consent was given. However, if subsequently a patient denies that he agreed to the injection, and merely moved his head because his neck was aching, it would not be easy for the nurse to dispute the fact that consent was not given. The nurse could point to other non-verbal communication such as the patient holding out his arm and rolling up a sleeve, as all such actions would suggest non-verbal agreement. Also, failure on the patient's part to stop the injection would indicate that there was agreement. The nurse is clearly in a more vulnerable position than if he/she had consent in writing.

The term 'implied consent' is sometimes incorrectly used. For example, it is sometimes suggested that by coming into hospital the patient has given an implied consent to the treatment and care provided. It would be dangerous to rely upon such an assumption because there are so many choices in treatment and care that it would be difficult to show that the patient had given consent to one particular form of treatment rather than another. It has also been suggested that when a patient is unconscious and brought into hospital following a road accident, then he/she is implying consent to being treated (*Mohr v. Williams*, 1905). A preferable view to take is that where a patient is unconscious, without any advance statement of directions, he implies nothing, and health professionals act on a different basis in law: the common law power to act out of necessity in the best interests of a mentally incapacitated person (*F. v. West Berkshire Health Authority and another* [1989]; *Chapter 7*).

Consent to screening

The same principles which apply to consent to treatment, also apply to patient participation in screening or in agreeing to undergo tests. When blood is taken to be tested, then the mentally competent patient must give consent to that blood being taken and also be given information about the use which will be made of that sample. Difficulties have arisen with testing for HIV. In practice, a distinction has been made between anonymous testing when the test result is not linked back to a specific patient and testing where the individual patient is told the result. In the latter case, the patient should receive counselling before giving consent to his or her blood being tested for HIV antibodies. The Public Health Laboratory Service commenced a programme of anonymous HIV antibody testing, using blood left over from other tests authorised by the patient. A UKCC Registrar's letter (12/93) dated 6 April 1993 sets guidelines for practitioners involved in such testing and implicitly supported such testing provided that it was on an anonymous basis for epidemiological purposes.

In December 1998 the Government launched a campaign to encourage all pregnant women to have an HIV test. The press release stated that only 30% of women who are HIV positive are aware that they are infected. If a pregnant woman is known to be HIV positive, then the risk of passing on HIV to the fetus can be reduced by arranging for delivery to be by Caesarean section. Avoiding breast feeding also removes the risk of passing on the virus through the milk. However, the law has not been changed and a test for HIV still requires the consent of the woman. The Government set a national target to achieve an 80% reduction by December 2002 in the number of children who acquire HIV from their mothers (HSC 1999/183).

In its HIV/AIDS Services 2000/2001 allocation and strategy, NHS organisations were instructed that part of the HIV prevention budget was to be used to support antenatal services in recommending an HIV test to all pregnant women. A research project to estimate the cost effectiveness of a universal, voluntary HIV screening programme has suggested that it is effective and should be implemented in the London area, with other areas being considered for screening (Postma MJ *et al* (1999)).

DNA fingerprints

There had been controversy over whether the police were entitled to keep fingerprints and DNA information about individuals who have been acquitted or ceased to be suspected of criminal offences. The Court of Appeal ruled on 12 September 2002 that police could keep DNA and fingerprints from unconvicted suspects. It held that the present procedure complied with the European Convention on Human Rights.

Box 3.2: Case scenario

Mary's consultant is correct in that if Mary has given him, in the outpatients' consultation, consent to have a biopsy and, if necessary, to follow the biopsy with a radical mastectomy, then that is valid in law. It is assumed that Mary had the necessary mental capacity, that there was no compulsion, and that she was clearly informed about the biopsy and when a radical mastectomy might be the preferred treatment. If the consultant is correct in his recollection, then there has been consent by Mary to both the biopsy and the radical mastectomy. It has to be assumed that Mary has not withdrawn the consent which she gave by word of mouth and it is reasonable to rely upon it. However, the consultant is in a vulnerable position if, having undertaken a radical mastectomy, Mary denies that she had agreed to the full operation. She may say that she had only agreed to come into hospital for the biopsy. She had planned, if there was malignancy, to have chemotherapy and radiotherapy and to avoid any major surgery. It may be that a nurse in the outpatient department recollected the conversation or the consultant may have recorded in his medical records that Mary was to have a biopsy and, if necessary, a radical mastectomy. However, if Mary denies that she ever gave consent, and is adamant that she intended to pursue other courses of treatment, then it would be very difficult for the consultant to refute her evidence. He would be in a much stronger position if he had the written consent by Mary to both the biopsy and, should it prove necessary, the radical mastectomy.

While the surgeon might be prepared to take the risk of proceeding on his recollection of what was said in outpatients, the theatre sister would be wise to insist that the surgeon should not proceed and postpone the surgery for later that day. It might be suggested that if Mary has only had the preoperative medication, and has not been anaesthetised, then she could sign the consent form there and then. However, this ignores the fact that Mary, as a result of that medication, may not have the mental capacity to understand what may happen and give a clear consent. It would be much wiser not to rely on any written consent which is signed after the preoperative medication has been given.

While this may subsequently infuriate Mary, the wisest course of action is for the surgeon and nurses to accept that they need to have Mary's consent in writing to what is proposed and to ask for her to be returned to the ward. When she has recovered from the preoperative injection she must be told about what is intended and given the opportunity to sign the consent form.

Clearly, apologies and explanations would have to be given to Mary as to why she was brought back from theatre, but it is a lesson to the ward staff that they should not have given Mary the preoperative medication until they had checked that a valid consent in writing was present among the records. Hopefully, Mary's fury and the inconvenience to ward and theatre staff would prevent such a reoccurrence and ensure that an appropriate procedure was implemented in future.

Conclusions

This chapter has considered the documentation which should show evidence that consent has been given. In the next chapter we consider how much information should be given to patients or parents.

References

Department of Health (1999) *HSC 1999/183 Reducing mother to baby transmission of HIV*. DoH, London

Department of Health (2001a) *Reference Guide to Consent for Examination or Treatment*. DoH, London; online at: http://www.doh.gov.uk/consent

Department of Health (2001b) *Good practice in consent implementation guide*. DoH, London: November

F. v. *West Berkshire Health Authority and another* [1989] 2 All ER 545; *Re F. (mental patient: sterilization)* [1990] 2 AC 1

Mohr v. *Williams* (1905) 104 NW (Sup Ct Minn) Judge Brown

Postma MJ *et al* (1999) Universal HIV screening of pregnant women in England: cost effectiveness analysis. *Br Med J* **318**: 1656–60

Sidaway v. *Bethlem Royal Hospital Governors* [1985] 1 All ER 643, [1985] AC 871

UKCC Registrar's letter (12/93) dated 6 April 1993

4

The duty of care to inform

In this chapter, we consider the law and cases relating to the duty of care to inform. The next chapter will consider some of the problems in implementing this duty.

The duty of care

If a valid consent by a mentally competent person has been given for a particular procedure, then that will be a defence against a possible action for trespass to the person. The patient may allege that he/she was not told about specific risks associated with the procedure. If these risks subsequently occur and harm is caused and the patient can show that he/she would not have agreed to the procedure had he/she known of these risks, then he/she may succeed in an action for negligence against the professional or the professional's employer. The latter is vicariously liable for any negligence by its employees committed in the course of their employment. Unlike an action for trespass to the person, where harm does not have to be established, an action for negligence will only succeed if harm can be shown. As in any other action for negligence, there are four elements which the claimant will have to establish:

- a duty of care is owed by the defendant (or the defendant's employee), including the duty to inform
- there has been a breach of this duty of care by a failure to follow the reasonable standard of care, as defined in the Bolam Test (*Bolam* v. *Friern Hospital Management Committee* [1957])
- a reasonably foreseeable consequence of this breach of duty is that
- harm has occurred as a result.

All four elements must be established by the claimant on a balance of probabilities. These elements in an action for negligence will be considered in relation to the giving of information to the patient.

Withholding information

The other question which arises is: in what circumstances, if any, could information be withheld from the patient? This is considered below.

Chatterton v. *Gerson*

A case where the clear distinction was drawn between an action for trespass to the person and an action for breach of the duty of care to inform was the case of *Chatterton* v. *Gerson* [1981]. In this case, Judge Bristow said:

> *In my judgement, once the patient is informed in broad terms of the nature of the procedure which is intended, and gives her consent, that consent is real, and the cause of the action on which to base a claim for failure to go into risks and implications is negligence, not trespass.*

The duty of care

The duty of care to diagnose, advise and treat also includes the duty to inform the patient. The courts have held that the duty of care is not divisible: it includes all the above components (*Sidaway* v. *Bethlem Royal Hospital Governors* [1985]).

The standard of care

How much information are doctors, nurses and other health professionals expected to give the patient? In America, there is a concept of informed consent, and it is a requirement that any relevant information in the knowledge of the health professionals should be given to a patient before consent is given to a particular procedure.

In the Sidaway case (*Sidaway* v. *Bethlem Royal Hospital Governors* [1985]), the House of Lords held that the English Courts do not recognise a concept of informed consent. The facts of this case were that Amy Sidaway agreed to undergo an operation to relieve pain in her neck. She was informed about the possibility of disturbing a root nerve, but not about the risk of damage to the spinal cord. Unfortunately, the latter occurred and she became severely disabled. She sued for negligence on the basis that there was a breach of the duty of care to inform her about the possibility of such a risk.

The trial judge held that the surgeon had told her about the possibility of damage to the nerve root, and that he had not told her of the danger of damage to the spinal cord (the aggregate risk of damage to the nerve root or spinal cord occurring was estimated at between one and two per cent), nor did he tell her that it was an operation of choice rather than necessity.

However, in refraining from informing her of these facts, he was following a practice at that time (1974) which would have been accepted as proper by a responsible body of skilled and experienced neurosurgeons. The judge thus applied what has become known as the Bolam Test (*Bolam* v. *Friern Hospital Management Committee* [1957]) to the case. In this case Judge McNair stated that:

> *The standard of care was that of the ordinary skilled man exercising and professing to have that special skill... A doctor was not guilty of negligence if he acted in accordance with the practice accepted at that time as proper by a responsible body of medical opinion, notwithstanding that other doctors adopted different practices.*

As a consequence, Amy Sidaway lost her case in the High Court and appealed to the Court of Appeal unsuccessfully and thence to the House of Lords. The judges in the House of Lords all had different bases for their views, but they agreed that in general she had failed in her action. Lord Diplock applied the Bolam Test to the duty of care to inform. Lord Bridge distinguished between two extremes: warning the patient of all possible risks once the treatment has been decided upon in the patient's best interests, and not warning the patient of any risks in order not to alarm the patient. Between these two extremes, Lord Bridge suggested that the Bolam Test should be applied, but this did not mean handing over to the medical profession the entire question of the scope of the duty of disclosure. There will be circumstances where the judge could come to the conclusion that disclosure of a particular risk was so obviously necessary to an informed choice on the part of the patient that no reasonably prudent medical person would fail to make it.

Lord Templeman stated that:

> *In my opinion, if a patient knows that a major operation may entail serious consequences, the patient cannot complain of lack of information unless the patient asks in vain for more information or unless there is some danger which by its nature or magnitude or for some other reason required to be separately taken into account by the patient in order to reach a balanced judgement in deciding whether or not to submit to the operation.*

Lord Scarman supported a 'prudent patient test', a concept derived from an American case, *Canterbury* v. *Spence* 464 F 2d 772 (DC, 1972). In this case, it was recognised that there were four principles, as listed in *Table 4.1*.

Bolam Test

The Bolam Test does not assume that there is only one way to inform patients or to carry out treatment procedures. As McNair said, 'a doctor was not guilty of negligence if he acted in accordance with the practice accepted at that time as proper by a responsible body of medical opinion, notwithstanding that other doctors adopted different practices.'

This conforms with the ruling given by the House of Lords in the Maynard case (*Maynard* v. *W Midlands Regional Health Authority* HL 1985) where the House of Lords emphasised that:

> *It was not sufficient to establish negligence for the plaintiff (ie. claimant) to show that there was a body of competent professional opinion that considered the decision was wrong, if there was also a body of equally competent professional opinion that supported the decision as having been reasonable in the circumstances.*

The House of Lords (*Bolitho* v. *City Hospital Hackney*) has urged that experts must give responsible and reasonable evidence (see below). In the case of *Smith* v. *Tunbridge Wells Health Authority* it was held that even though some surgeons were not providing warnings of the risk of a rectal prolapse, it was neither reasonable nor responsible for the surgeon in that particular case, who was therefore held to be in breach of the duty of care to inform.

Table 4.1: The four principles of the *Canterbury* v. *Spence* 464 F 2d 772 (DC, 1972) case

1. Every human being of adult years and of sound mind has a right to determine what shall be done with his/her own body.

2. The consent is the informed exercise of a choice, and that entails an opportunity to evaluate knowledgeably the options available and the risks attendant on each.

3. The doctor must therefore disclose all 'material risks'. What risks are 'material' is determined by the 'prudent patient' test, which is as follows: a risk is... material when a reasonable person, in what the physician knows or should know to be the patient's position, would be likely to attach significance to the risk or cluster of risks in deciding whether or not to forgo the proposed therapy.

4. The doctor has, however, a therapeutic privilege. This exception is that a reasonable medical assessment of the patient would have indicated to the doctor that disclosure would have posed a serious threat of psychological detriment to the patient.

Gold v. *Haringey Health Authority* [1988]

The principles set by the House of Lords in the Sidaway case were followed in *Gold* v. *Haringey*. In this case, following a sterilisation the patient became pregnant with her fourth child. She sued for negligence alleging that she should have been warned of the failure rate of female sterilisations and had she been told, her husband would have had a vasectomy. Evidence was given that at that time (1979) a competent body of professional opinion would not have given a warning. The judge held that this test only applied to advice in a therapeutic context and not to a warning in a contraceptive situation and found for the claimant. The Court of Appeal held that there was no distinction in law between advice given in a therapeutic context and a non-therapeutic context and the Bolam Test applied to both diagnosis, treatment and the giving of advice.

The Pearce case

The situation set out in the case scenario (*Box 4.1*) is an actual situation and a decided case (*Pearce* v. *United Bristol Healthcare NHS Trust*, 1998). The trial judge dismissed Mrs Pearce's claim, holding that there had been no negligence on the part of the consultant in not advising Mrs Pearce of the small risk attached to waiting for natural labour to begin.

The Court of Appeal held that the experts had agreed that the risk of the child being stillborn was not a significant risk — possibly 0.1–0.2%. The Court of Appeal stated that it would not interfere with the clinical opinion of the expert medical man responsible for treating Mrs Pearce. It accepted that there would be occasions in which the courts could decide that the expert opinion is not acceptable to the court.

In this, the court was following the ruling in the Bolitho case

(*Bolitho* v. *City and Hackney HA* [1997]), where the House of Lords held that there would be occasions where the courts could find that expert opinion presented to it was not acceptable. The House of Lords held that:

> *The use of the adjectives 'responsible, reasonable and respectable' (in the Bolam case) all showed that the court had to be satisfied that the exponents of the body of opinion relied upon could demonstrate that such opinion had a logical basis.*

Overruling experts was seen, however, as an extreme situation:

> *It would seldom be right for a judge to reach the conclusion that views held by a competent medical expert were unreasonable.*

Future developments

There would appear to be a development in favour of greater openness between professional and patient, with the presumption in favour of the patient having all relevant information. While the UK courts have not accepted that a doctrine of informed consent is recognised in law, ethical practice is placing more emphasis on the rights of the patient to be given as much information as possible. It may be that in the future there will be statutory provisions over what the patient should be told. For example, explanatory leaflets must be provided by pharmaceutical companies as a result of a European Directive (European Directive 92/27/EEC). It may be an area where the recommendations of the National Institute of Clinical Excellence (NICE) cover the information given to patients. The Kennedy report (2001) made clear recommendations on the giving of information to patients. These are shown in *Box 4.2* (see also *Box 2.4* and *Box 5.4*).

Box 4.2: Recommendations on information giving in the Kennedy report

4. Information about treatment and care should be given in a variety of forms, be given in stages and be reinforced over time.
5. Information should be tailored to the needs, circumstances and wishes of the individual.
6. Information should be based on the current available evidence and include a summary of the evidence and data, in a form which is comprehensible to patients.
7. Various modes of conveying information, whether leaflets, tapes, videos or CDs, should be regularly updated and developed and piloted with the help of patients.
8. The NHS Modernisation Agency should make the improvement of the quality of information for patients a priority. In relation to the consent and dissemination of information for patients, the Agency should identify and promote a good practice throughout the NHS. It should establish a system for accrediting materials intended to inform patients.
9. The public should receive guidance on those sources of information about health and health care on the Internet which are reliable and of good quality: a kite-marking system should be developed.
26. As part of the process of obtaining consent, except when they have indicated otherwise, patients should be given sufficient information about what is to take place, the risks, uncertainties, and possible negative consequences of the proposed treatment, about any alternatives and about the likely outcome, to enable them to make a choice about how to proceed.

Conclusion

Although the judges in the House of Lords in the Sidaway case all had different reasons for their decision to dismiss Mrs Sidaway's appeal, it is possible to make the following statement in the light of the more recent House of Lords decision in the Bolitho case.

The courts have the right to decide if they consider that the expert opinion on the standard of disclosure is acceptable to the courts. They will require a patient to be informed of significant risks according to the reasonable standard of medical practice (ie. Bolam), but that this will be subject to the duty to ensure that the patient is notified of any serious risk which a prudent patient would be expected to want to know.

The implications of this will be considered in the next chapter when these legal rulings will be applied to practical questions frequently faced by health professionals.

References

Bolam v. *Friern Hospital Management Committee* [1957] 1 WLR 582

Bolitho v. *City and Hackney HA* [1997] 4 All ER 771

Canterbury v. *Spence* 464 F 2d 772 (DC, 1972)

Chatterton v. *Gerson* [1981] QB 432

European Directive 92/27/EEC (L113/8)

Kennedy I (2001) Bristol Royal Infirmary Inquiry Learning from Bristol: the report of the public inquiry into children's heart surgery at the Bristol Royal Infirmary 1984–1995. Command paper CM 5207. Stationery Office, London

Gold v. *Haringey Health Authority* [1988] 1 QB 481

Maynard v. *W Midlands Regional Health Authority* HL [1985] 1 All ER 635

Pearce v. *United Bristol Healthcare NHS Trust* (1998) 48 BMLR 118 CA; [1999] PIQR P53 CA

Sidaway v. *Bethlem Royal Hospital Governors* [1985] 1 All ER 643, [1985] AC 871

Smith v. *Tunbridge Wells Health Authority* [1994] 5 Med LR 334

5

The duty to inform patients of risks

Box 5.1: Case scenario, scared stiff

Fred has suffered for many years with a hernia and has been placed on the waiting list for surgery. He is finally admitted, but is extremely frightened, never having had any contact with hospitals before. He keeps asking about what will happen to him. Nurses discover that his mother died when he was only eight following an operation for the removal of gall stones. He is afraid that the same thing will happen to him.

In the last chapter we considered the cases which set down the principles which apply to the duty to inform the patient, noting that a modified Bolam Test (*Bolam* v. *Friern Hospital Management Committee* [1957]) was now the basic principle, ie. that health professionals should inform patients according to the reasonable standards recognised by the accepted practice, but that this was subject to oversight by the courts. Patients should be notified of significant risks that are likely to cause substantial harm. However, practitioners could withhold information if disclosure poses a serious threat of psychological detriment to the patient.

The Court of Appeal has considered how much information should be given to the patient in a recent case. The facts are shown in *Box 5.2*.

> ### Box 5.2: *Chester* v. *Afshar* The Times Law Report 13 June 2002; [2002] 3 All ER 552 CA
>
> The patient suffered from severe back pain and gave consent to an operation for the removal of three intra-vertebral discs. The patient alleged that the neurosurgeon failed to give a warning to her about the slight risk of post-operative paralysis which the patient suffered following the operation. This was denied by the neurosurgeon. The trial judge held that the doctor was not negligent in his conduct of the operation, but was negligent in failing to warn her of the slight risk of paralysis which she suffered and gave judgement for damages to be assessed. The defendant appealed against this finding of failing to give the appropriate information to the Court of Appeal.

The Court of Appeal held that the purpose of the rule requiring doctors to give appropriate information to their patients was to enable the patient to exercise her right to choose whether or not to have the particular operation to which she was asked to give her consent. The patient had the right to choose what would and would not be done with her body and the doctor should take the care expected of a reasonable doctor in the circumstances in giving her the information relevant to that choice. The law was designed to require doctors properly to inform their patients of the risk attendant on their treatment and to answer questions put to them as to that treatment and its dangers, such answers to be judged in the context of good professional practice, which had tended to a greater degree of frankness over the years, with more respect being given to patient autonomy.

The object was to enable the patient to decide whether or not to run the risks of having that operation at that time. If the doctor's failure to take care resulted in her consenting to an operation to which she would not otherwise have given her consent, the purpose of that rule would be thwarted if he were not to be held responsible when the risk about which he failed to warn her materialised and caused her an injury.

The outcome was that the appeal by the surgeon against the finding of negligence failed and the patient won the case. At the time of writing an appeal is to go to the House of Lords on the issue of causation, ie. did the doctor's failure to warn cause harm to the patient.

Case of *Chinchen* v. *University Hospital of Wales Healthcare NHS Trust* (Chinchen 2002)

In this case a patient underwent surgery for revision decompression of his spine. The facts are shown in *Box 5.3*. He claimed that he was not given proper advice before the decompression procedure. Had he received proper advice, he would not have consented to that procedure. The judge found in favour of C. The reasons for the judge's decision are shown in *Box 5.4*. The case shows the importance of which side can prove what was actually said before the patient agreed to undergo the operation.

> **Box 5.3: *Chinchen* v. *University Hospital of Wales Healthcare NHS Trust* 2002 (facts)**
>
> In April 1996, C. underwent surgery for a revision decompression of his spine. A consultant orthopaedic surgeon carried out the procedure. Four days later, C. suffered loss of spinal fluid from the operation wound and was readmitted to hospital. In May a posterior exploration of C.'s lower lumbar spine was carried out. The dura was inspected and there was no obvious leak. A muscle patch was applied to the dura and C. was later discharged home. C. suffered constant and debilitating pain and an inability to return to work after the procedures and claimed that he was not given proper advice before the decompression procedure. Had he received proper advice, he would not have consented to that procedure.

Box 5.4: *Chinchen* v. *University Hospital of Wales Healthcare NHS Trust* 2002 (reasons)

The judge preferred C.'s recollections of the pre-operative discussion. Both C. and his wife's version were the same, they were convincing witnesses, and they had the benefit of consulting solicitors no later than a year after the operation and so events were fresh in their minds. The surgeon's evidence had changed and he had been in a difficult position, as he had not had to try and recall the events until four years after the operation. On the evidence, C. had not been advised of alternative procedures, nor had he been warned of the possible risks consequent upon undergoing revision surgery. The surgeon had conveyed assurances that it would be fine and C. had not been told that the surgery was urgent. The advice given did not satisfy the minimal standards of professional competence. There should have been a clear warning of the higher incidence of problems arising from revision surgery and other options should have been discussed. The surgeon admitted that he had not explained to C. that any course of action was available other than surgery. In the instant circumstances, had C. received the appropriate advice he would not have agreed to undergo the operation. The judge found that there was a causal and temporal connection between the surgery and the symptoms, which were different and worse very soon after the surgery. The two operations had occurred within a short period on a site previously operated upon and had caused damage resulting in C.'s operation. The symptoms were much worse than they would have been without the surgery.

Common questions

How much do I tell the patient?

Any health practitioner who is caring for a patient should ensure that the patient is aware of any significant risks of substantial harm. For example, a nurse may be asked by the patient what is going to happen, even though the patient has signed the consent form. The patient's question would appear to suggest that the patient has not had a clear explanation of the proposed procedure. The nurse may be able to answer the question herself, but only if she has kept up-to-date with research and the treatment proposed. If she does not have the knowledge to answer the patient's questions she should ask the doctor or other health professional concerned to return and give the patient the information required. Where possible, the health professional should attempt to ensure that information for the patient is put in writing as well as being given to the patient by word of mouth. This gives the patient the opportunity to look over the information sheet at leisure and also has the additional advantage of providing some evidence that the patient was informed of specific risks described in the leaflet.

When is a risk significant?

A risk is significant if it is the kind of information which a reasonable patient would want to know before agreeing to a particular treatment. The courts have been reluctant to rely on risk percentages and have not laid down any principle, eg. that all risks higher than 10% should be notified to the patient. When assessing the significance of a risk it has to be linked with the extent of the harm. Clearly, even a small risk of a devastating disability will be more material to the decision-making processes of the patient, than a large risk of minimal harm. For example, a 1% risk of paralysis will be of more concern than a 50% risk of a temporary headache.

What if the patient asks questions?

Lord Bridge suggested in the Sidaway case *(Sidaway* v. *Bethlem Royal Hospital Governors* [1985]) that if the patient asked questions, then the doctor has a duty to answer these truthfully and as fully as the questions require. Lord Diplock stated:

> *No doubt if the patient in fact manifested this attitude (ie. wanted to decide for themselves what should be done to them) by means of questioning, the doctor would tell him whatever it was the patient wanted to know.'*

What if the patient does not ask questions?

If the patient does not appear to want more information, provided that the health professional has informed the patient of the basic information according to the Bolam Test, there would appear to be no duty to continue to provide all the additional information which may be sought by a particularly informed and interested patient. Many health professionals are familiar with patients who say, 'whatever you recommend nurse, doctor, etc.' and who appear not to want to have much information about their condition, treatment or prognosis. However, patients should be given any available leaflet, whether they are likely to read it or not, so that the health professional can fulfil his/her duty to inform.

In the Blyth case *(Blyth* v. *Bloomsbury HA* [1993]), in the Court of Appeal, Lord Justice Kerr held that:

> *The question of what a plaintiff should be told in answer to a general enquiry cannot be divorced from the Bolam Test, any more than when no such enquiry is made. In both cases, the answer must depend upon the circumstances, the nature of the enquiry, the nature of the information which is available, its reliability, relevance, the condition of the patient, and so*

forth. Any medical evidence directed to what would be the proper answer in the light of responsible medical opinion and practice — that is to say, the Bolam Test — must in my view equally be placed in the balance in cases where the patient makes some enquiry, in order to decide whether the response was negligent or not.

When can I withhold information?

In the case scenario (*Box 5.1*), it is clear that Fred is nervous. Although his hernia repair operation may be attended by very little risk, it may be that notifying him of any risks will deter him from having the operation. The fact that his mother died during an operation should be taken into account in assessing Fred's suitability for surgery and all necessary tests should be undertaken. For example, it may be that his mother died because of an allergic response to the anaesthetic and this could be a hereditary condition. If so, it is essential that Fred is tested for any such allergy before the operation. Such additional precautions may assist in reassuring Fred about the dangers of the operation so that he is able to give consent. However, he may still ask questions about the possibility of different kinds of risks. A professional judgement then has to be made as to whether such information is counterproductive and should be withheld from Fred.

In a sense this is paternalistic practice, but there is a substantial legal justification for such withholding of information (*Sidaway* v. *Bethlem Royal Hospital Governors* [1985]).

Also, legislation such as the Data Protection Act 1998 and the regulations for access to health records made under it, recognise that access to records can be withheld where such access would cause serious harm to the physical or mental health or condition of the patient. The patient does not have an absolute right to access his/her health records or to obtain information.

However, any withholdings should be the exception rather than the rule and should be clearly defensible. It is also highly recommended that the fact and reasons for the withholding should be clearly documented, so that, in the event of a patient challenging the fact that this information was not given, the reasons are clearly recorded.

What if more information is available because of research being conducted locally?

This question was raised in *Blyth* v. *Bloomsbury HA* [1993]. Mrs Blyth brought an action against the health authority on the grounds that she had been given negligent advice and information. She had been administered the contraceptive drug Depo-Provera by injection and claimed that she had suffered unpleasant side-effects. She alleged that had she been informed about the possible side-effects more fully, she would not have agreed to have the injection. The trial judge held that there was an obligation to give the plaintiff all the information available to the hospital, including information in the files of a consultant who had studied the subject. This, however, was overruled by the Court of Appeal which held that there was no such obligation.

Case scenario

Fred presents a difficult case. His fear should not be used to justify withholding information about significant risks of substantial harm. If he is a mentally competent person, and on the facts given here it would appear that there is no suggestion to the contrary, he needs to be questioned about what happened to his mother to ensure that he is not at risk from a genetic defect and encouraged to undergo all the necessary tests to check out reasonably foreseeable risks. His questions must be answered fully and truthfully and he should be given all the information with which similar patients are provided, and if possible, in writing. Health professionals should ensure that they have followed the reasonable standard of care in informing Fred about the operation and its after effects. Documentation should record such discussions and the handing out of leaflets giving details of the treatment and risks associated with it.

Guidance

This is a difficult area and health professionals should be aware of the guidance which is available not only from their own professional registration bodies, but also from professional associations. In addition, standards on the giving of information to patients before the consent is signed have been laid down by the Clinical Negligence Scheme for Trusts (CNST). The standards will be monitored as part of the CNST's administration of the pool for paying out claims arising from clinical negligence. The Department of Health has issued a reference guide on consent to treatment (DoH, 2001a), together with practical guidance on the implementation of the principles (DoH, 2001b) which has been noted in earlier chapters. The Kennedy report (2001) has made significant recommendations on communications with patients. Some of its recommendations on information giving are shown in *Box 4.2*. *Table 5.1* sets out the Kennedy recommendations on communication with patients.

Table 5.1: Recommendations of the Kennedy report on communications with patients	
10.	Tape-recording facilities should be provided by the NHS to enable patients, should they so wish, to make a tape recording of a discussion with a healthcare professional when a diagnosis, course of treatment, or prognosis is being discussed.
11.	Patients should always be given the opportunity and time to ask questions about what they are told, to seek clarification and to ask for more information. It must be the responsibility of employers in the NHS to ensure that the working arrangements of healthcare professionals allow for this, not least that they have the necessary time.
12.	Patients must be given such information as enables them to participate in their care.
13.	Before embarking on any procedure, patients should be given an explanation of what is going to happen and, after the procedure, should have the opportunity to review what has happened.
14.	Patients should be supported in dealing with the additional anxiety sometimes created by greater knowledge.
15.	Patients should be told that they may have another person of their choosing present when receiving information about a diagnosis or a procedure.
16.	Patients should be given the sense of freedom to indicate when they do not want any (or more) information: this requires skill and understanding from healthcare professionals.
17.	Patients should receive a copy of any letter written about their care or treatment by one healthcare professional to another.
19.	Healthcare professionals responsible for the care of any particular patient must communicate effectively with each other. The aim must be to avoid giving the patient conflicting advice and information.
20.	The provision of counselling and support should be regarded as an integral part of a patient's care. All hospital trusts should have a well-developed system and a well-trained group of professionals whose task it is to provide this type of support and to make links to various other forms of support (such as that provided by voluntary or social services) which patients may need.
33.	A duty of candour, meaning a duty to tell a patient if adverse events have occurred, must be recognised as owed by all those working in the NHS to patients.
34.	When things go wrong, patients are entitled to receive an acknowledgement, an explanation and an apology.

Conclusions

Honesty and respect are at the heart of a good system of communications with patients, and any withholding of information should be based on sound justification and clearly documented. The recommendations of the Bristol Inquiry shown in *Table 5.1* have significant resource and training implications. However, it is essential that trusts work to this high standard of communication with patients. The presumption is in favour of ensuring that the mentally competent patient is fully informed of the proposed treatment and care and its risks and side-effects. Account must be taken of the differing abilities of patients in understanding the information and use made of a wide variety of types of communication.

References

Blyth v. *Bloomsbury HA* [1993] 4 Med LR 151 CA

Bolam v. *Friern Hospital Management Committee* [1957] 1 WLR 582

Chester v. *Afshar* The Times Law Report 13 June 2002; [2002] 3 All ER 552 CA

Chinchen v. *University Hospital of Wales Healthcare NHS Trust* 8 November 2001 (Current Law 340 April 2002)

Department of Health (2001a) *Reference Guide to Consent for Examination or Treatment*. DoH, London; online at: http://www.doh.gov.uk/consent

Department of Health (2001b) *Good practice in consent implementation guide*. DoH, London: November

Kennedy I (2001) Bristol Royal Infirmary Inquiry Learning from Bristol: the report of the public inquiry into children's heart surgery at the Bristol Royal Infirmary 1984–1995. Command paper CM 5207. Stationery Office, London

Sidaway v. *Bethlem Royal Hospital Governors* [1985] 1 All ER 643, [1985] AC 871

6

The determination of mental capacity

Box 6.1: Case scenario one

Doctors advised a patient (C.) from Broadmoor Special Hospital, who was suffering from chronic paranoid schizophrenia, that he had gangrene in his foot. He was transferred to Heatherwood Hospital where the doctor diagnosed a grossly infected right leg with a necrotic ulcer covering the whole of the dorsum. The consultant vascular surgeon considered that C. would die immediately unless he had a below-knee amputation. His chances of survival were assessed as being no better than 15% if he just had conservative treatment. C. stated that he would prefer to die with two feet than live with one. He therefore refused to give consent to the operation and he sought an injunction from the High Court to stop the amputation from going ahead (*Re C. (adult: refusal of medical treatment)* [1984]).

In the second chapter of this book, it was stated that in order to be valid, consent must be given by a person who has the necessary mental capacity. This chapter seeks to explore what is meant by 'capacity' and how this can be determined in individual circumstances.

Presumption of mental capacity

The law presumes that an adult has the mental capacity to make a valid decision and has the right of self-determination. This is the starting point in determining whether an individual's refusal is binding upon health professionals. However, evidence can be brought to refute this presumption.

In 1995, the Law Commission (an independent body which reviews UK laws) published its report *Mental Incapacity* (Law Commission Mental Capacity, 1995) which followed five years of consultation and consultation papers on all aspects of mentally incapacitated adults. This report (Paragraph 3.14) used the following definition of mental incapacity:

> *A person is without capacity if at the material time he/she is: unable by reason of mental disability to make a decision on the matter in question; or*
> *unable to communicate a decision on that matter because he/she is unconscious or for any other reason.*

In terms of the level of understanding, Paragraph 3.18 recommended that:

> *A person should not be regarded as unable to understand the information relevant to a decision if he or she is able to understand an explanation of that information in broad terms and simple language.*

The three-stage test of mental capacity

In case scenario one, the sole issue before Mr Justice Thorpe was did C. have the requisite capacity to give a valid refusal, ie. was his right of self-determination to be upheld? If the answer to the question was 'yes', then he had the right in law to refuse any treatment, 'for a good reason, a bad reason or for no reason at all' (words used by the Court of Appeal in *Re MB. (an adult: medical treatment)* (1997)). On the other hand, if the effect of his chronic paranoid schizophrenia was to render him incapable of making a valid decision, then action could be taken in his best interests and his refusal overruled.

Mr Justice Thorpe stated that there were three stages in determining whether the requisite mental capacity existed:

- could the patient comprehend and retain the necessary information?
- was he able to believe it?
- was he able to weigh the information, balancing risks and needs, so as to arrive at a choice?

Could the patient comprehend and retain the necessary information?

The importance of this first stage in determining competence can be seen when considering the capacity of patients who suffer from a disease such as Alzheimer's disease, where there is intermittent competence and the patient may appear at one point to be understanding what is said but then forget that information almost immediately afterwards.

Was he able to believe it?

Patients who are paranoid might not be able to believe the facts which are placed before them. This test was not specifically included in the test of mental capacity laid down by the Court of Appeal in Re MB. (see *page 98*).

Was he able to weigh the information, balancing risks and needs, so as to arrive at a choice?

This last stage requires cognitive abilities to make a decision on the basis of the information presented.

Non-supportable or irrational decisions

None of these three stages include agreeing with the patient's choice. The fact that others might disagree with the person's decision or the person is not necessarily acting in their own best interests is not a determinant of mental capacity.

As the Law Commission recommended (paragraph 3.19):

A person should not be regarded as unable to make a decision by reason of mental disability merely because he or she makes a decision which would not be made by a person of ordinary prudence.

If a requisite of the decision-making process was that the patient made a decision that health professionals agreed with, then those who are Jehovah's Witnesses would find that they could not refuse blood. Self-determination is the opposite of paternalism. Health professionals may find it difficult to accept when a mentally competent patient refuses life-saving treatment, but that is the patient's right in law. It follows that provided that the patient is defined as having the mental capacity to make a decision, according to the approved tests, the fact that the decision is irrational or unwise or contrary to the best interests of the patient, is not relevant. This is the ruling of the case of *Re MB. (an adult: medical treatment)* (1997) (see below and *Chapter 12*) and also of the recent case of *Re B. (consent to treatment: capacity)* 2002 (see below).

The capacity must relate to the decision to be made

There are different levels of decision making, eg. from deciding what clothes to wear, to deciding whether to have an operation or donate bone marrow. Those patients who suffer from learning disabilities may be able to make decisions on day-to-day matters, but may not have the capacity to be able to weigh the information, balancing risks and needs, so as to arrive at a choice for the more critical decisions.

Whether or not a patient has the capacity to make specific decisions is part of the risk assessment process which any treatment plan should include. Obviously, clear documentation of the analysis and the reasons for any decision on mental capacity should be kept.

Who determines capacity?

Box 6.2: Case scenario two

Fred has suffered for many years with a hernia and has been placed on the waiting list for surgery. He is finally admitted, but is extremely frightened never having had any contact with hospitals before. He keeps asking what will happen to him. Nurses discover that his mother died when he was only eight years old following an operation for the removal of gallstones. He is afraid that the same thing will happen to him.

'Case scenario two' appeared in the previous chapter. Let us assume that after all the tests had been conducted and all the information and reassurance given to Fred, he still decided that he would not have the operation. Should this refusal be overruled? The question then arises as to Fred's mental capacity to make a valid refusal.

There are considerable advantages in bringing in a specialist outside the clinical team caring for Fred. Preferably, this would be a psychologist whose training includes the determination of mental capacity. If the psychologist were to say that Fred's fear of the operation because of the death of his mother is such that it makes it impossible for him to make a valid decision, ie. his fear renders him mentally incapable, then it could be argued that his refusal is invalid and he could be treated as a mentally incapacitated adult and action taken in his best interests. In one case, the Court of Appeal agreed with the High Court's decision that a fear of needles meant that the patient was mentally incapable of making a decision and a Caesarean section could be performed in her best interests (*Re MB. (an adult: medical treatment)* (1997).

It does not follow that the operation must proceed. In Fred's case the operation is elective. It does not appear, on the facts, to be a life-saving necessity, so it is possible that an invalid refusal could prevail and Fred's refusal accepted. There would certainly seem to be strong reasons not to compel Fred to undergo surgery but instead to accept his refusal and, if subsequently surgical intervention did become a life-saving necessity, to reconsider the whole issue. (The question of the care of the person lacking mental capacity is considered in the next chapter.)

Could a member of the clinical team determine competence?

In practice, this happens in day-to-day matters. Every health practitioner is regularly deciding whether a person's presumption of self-determination is valid. Unfortunately, there is a tendency, particularly in the care of psychiatric patients, to assume that a passive acceptance of what is proposed by the health professionals indicates mental capacity, but when there is refusal to accept recommended treatment, then the capacity of the individual to refuse is questioned.

Clearly, if the situation is a life and death matter, as in the Broadmoor case of *Re C.*, then there are strong legal arguments why an expert should be brought in to examine the patient and determine his/her mental capacity. If the case does come before the courts, this will be the sole point at issue between the parties and evidence of the alleged incapacity will be required by the courts.

The Ms B. case

In *Chapter 2* we considered the case of Ms B. (*Re B.* 2002), who asked for her ventilator to be switched off. (The facts of the case are set out in *Chapter 2*.) The sole issue before the family court was whether Ms B. had the mental capacity to refuse life-saving treatment and care. The President of the Family Division, Dame Elizabeth Butler-Schloss restated the principles which had been laid down by the Court of Appeal in the case of St George's Healthcare Trust (St George's Healthcare Trust, 1998):

❖ There was a presumption that a patient had the mental capacity to make decisions whether to consent to or refuse medical or surgical treatment offered.
❖ If mental capacity was not an issue and the patient, having been given the relevant information and offered the available option, chose to refuse that treatment, that decision had to be respected by the doctors, considerations of what the best interests of the patient would involve were irrelevant.
❖ Concern or doubts about the patient's mental capacity should be resolved as soon as possible by the doctors within the hospital or other normal medical procedures.
❖ Meanwhile, the patient must be cared for in accordance with the judgement of the doctors as to the patient's best interests.

❖ It was most important that those considering the issue should not confuse the question of mental capacity with the nature of the decision made by the patient, however grave the consequences. Since the view of the patient might reflect a difference in values rather than an absence of competence, the assessment of capacity should be approached with that in mind and doctors should not allow an emotional reaction to, or strong disagreement with, the patient's decision to cloud their judgement in answering the primary question of capacity.

❖ Where disagreement still existed about competence, it was of the utmost importance that the patient be fully informed, involved and engaged in the process, which could involve obtaining independent outside help, of resolving the disagreement since the patient's involvement could be crucial to a good outcome.

❖ If the hospital was faced with a dilemma which doctors did not know how to resolve that must be recognised and further steps taken as a matter of priority. Those in charge must not allow a situation of deadlock or drift to occur.

❖ If there was no disagreement about competence, but the doctors were for any reason unable to carry out the patient's wishes it was their duty to find other doctors who would do so.

❖ If all appropriate steps to seek independent assistance from medical experts outside the hospital had failed, the hospital should not hesitate to make an application to the High Court or seek the advice of the Official Solicitor.

❖ The treating clinicians and the hospital should always have in mind that a seriously physically disabled patient who was mentally competent had the same right to personal autonomy and to make decisions as any other person with mental capacity.

Conclusion

When Mr Justice Thorpe applied the three-stage test to *Re C.*, it was decided that C. did have the mental capacity to refuse to give consent to the amputation and an injunction was issued forbidding any person to amputate his leg without his consent. This case shows that a person may suffer from a specific form of mental disorder, yet still have the requisite mental capacity to give or refuse consent. At the time of writing it is understood that C. is still alive.

References

Law Commission (1995) *Mental Incapacity*. Report No 231. HMSO, London

Re B. (consent to treatment: capacity) The Times Law Report 26 March 2002, [2002] 2 All ER 449

Re C. (adult: refusal of medical treatment) [1994] 1 WLR 290

Re MB. (an adult: medical treatment) (1997) 38 BMLR 175 CA

St George's Healthcare NHS Trust v. *S.* The Times 8 May 1998 [1999] Fam 26

7

The mentally incapacitated adult

> **Box 7.1: Case scenario**
>
> Bob Davies, aged seventy-five years, was admitted to hospital with what was thought to be an ulcerated hiatus hernia. The surgeon advised June, his only child, that with surgery he had a 60%–70% chance of a reasonable prognosis. Without an operation he was unlikely to survive because he was haemorrhaging badly. He asked June if she was prepared to give consent and sign the form.

Introduction

In the last chapter, the tests for determining mental capacity were discussed. This chapter considers the law which relates to the care of a person who lacks the necessary mental capacity to make a valid decision. If an adult lacks the mental capacity to make his/her decisions, then at present there is a vacuum in law. While parents can make decisions on behalf of their children until the children become adults at eighteen years (children can also make decisions in certain circumstances; the law on this is considered in the next two chapters), once a person is eighteen no-one has the right to give consent to treatment on his/her behalf.

Law Commission and statutory powers

In 1990, the Law Commission, an independent body which reviews our laws and suggests reforms, commenced a long consultation exercise to decide what laws we should have for decision making on behalf of and for the protection of mentally incapacitated adults. In 1995, it published its proposals (Law Commission, 1995) which included a draft Mental Incapacity Bill. This Bill proposed a statutory framework for decisions to be made on behalf of the mentally incapable adult, day-to-day decisions being made by a statutory decision maker, and special courts for making decisions in more complex situations such as abortions, sterilisations, etc. Unfortunately, the Government at the time did not place the Mental Incapacity Bill before Parliament so there was no legislation.

In December 1997, the Lord Chancellor issued a new consultation document (Lord Chancellor's Office, 1997) covering much of the ground already consulted upon by the Law Commission. Following this consultation, a White Paper (Lord Chancellor's Office, 1999) giving the Government's proposals on decision making on behalf of the mentally incapacitated adult was published in 1999. This follows the Law Commission's proposals, but there is no legislation proposed for advance refusals of treatment (living wills). A statutory duty to act in the best interests of the mentally incapacitated adult is proposed, with a new continuing power of attorney which could include treatment decisions, new courts which could make decisions in the more critical areas and to which applications could be made on behalf of the mentally incapacitated adult.

At the time of writing, legislation to enact the White Paper's proposals is still awaited. There is currently no Act of Parliament (for England, Wales and Northern Ireland) which provides for decision making on behalf of the mentally incapable adult in relation to treatment. In 2002, the Lord Chancellor's Department issued for consultation, leaflets about consent on behalf of specific patient groups.

(The Enduring Powers of Attorney Act 1985 does enable a person who has the necessary mental capacity to create a power of attorney to cover the time when he/she ceases to have the capacity, but this does not cover the delegation of powers to decide on treatment. The jurisdiction of the Court of Public Protection and the Public Trustee Office also do not cover treatment decisions.)

In Scotland, the Adults with Incapacity (Scotland) Act 2000 enables decisions to be made on behalf of mentally incapacitated adults. It covers both the making of medical decisions and also decisions relating to property and finance. The bulk of the provisions came into force in April 2002. The Act introduces a new regime of intervention and guardianship orders and reforms the law on powers of attorney. Former powers under the Mental Health (Scotland) Act 1984 are repealed. A new court jurisdiction is set up. The first section sets out the principles which are to apply including the principle that, 'there shall be no intervention in the affairs of an adult, unless the person responsible for authorising or effecting the intervention is satisfied that the intervention will benefit the adult and that such benefit cannot reasonably be achieved without the intervention.'

Common law powers

In the absence of statutory provision for decision making on behalf of mentally incapacitated adults, the courts have been obliged to fill the vacuum and lay down the principles which apply.

The leading case is *Re F.* (*Box 7.2*). In this case, the judge granted the declaration sought by F.'s mother. The Official Solicitor (who acts on behalf of the mentally incapacitated adult) appealed against the declaration to the Court of Appeal, which upheld the judge's order. The official solicitor then appealed to the House of Lords. The House of Lords held that there was at common law (ie. judge-made law or case law) the power for a person to act in the best interests of a mentally incapacitated adult. This power is derived from the principle of necessity.

> **Box 7.2: Sterilisation of a mentally incapacitated adult (*Re F. (mental patient: sterilisation)* [1990]**
>
> F. was thirty-six years old and had severe learning disabilities, with the mental age of a small child. She lived in a mental hospital and had formed a sexual relationship with a male patient. The hospital staff considered that she would be unable to cope with a pregnancy and recommended that she should be sterilised, considering that other forms of contraception were unsuitable. Her mother supported the idea of a sterilisation operation, but because F. was over eighteen years, she (ie. the mother) did not have the right in law to give consent on her behalf. The mother therefore applied to court for a declaration that an operation for sterilisation was in her best interests and should be declared lawful.

The principle of necessity

Necessity may arise in an emergency situation, eg. when an unconscious person comes into hospital, and the health professionals should do no more than is reasonably required in the best interests of the patient, before he/she recovers consciousness. Necessity may also arise in a situation where a person is permanently or semi-permanently lacking mental capacity. In such a situation, there is no point in waiting for the patient to give consent. According to Lord Goff:

> *The need to care for him [the patient] is obvious; and the doctor must then act in the best interests of his patient just as if he had received his consent so to do. Were this not so, much*

> *useful treatment and care could, in theory at least, be denied to the unfortunate.*

The doctor must act in accordance with a responsible and competent body of relevant professional opinion (*Bolam* v. *Friern Hospital Management Committee* [1957]).

The House of Lords issued a declaration that sterilisation was in the best interests of F. and could proceed. It did recommend that in future such cases of sterilisation for social reasons (as opposed, for example, to sterilisation which resulted from an operation to remove a cancerous growth) should be brought before the courts for a declaration to be made. How 'best interests' is defined by the courts is the subject of *Chapter 11*.

Decisions by relatives

Unfortunately, the situation in the 'case scenario' box (*Box 7.1*) is a frequent occurrence in hospitals, and yet in law June does not have the legal right to make such a decision on her father's behalf. She should not be invited to sign the consent form. Bob should make the decision, but if he is unable to do so, because he lacks the mental capacity or is unable to communicate his wishes, then the doctors have to decide what is in his best interests.

June's views should, of course, be sought, eg. does she have information about any previously declared wishes of Bob. If Bob had made a living will or advanced refusal of treatment this would apply. Where this is not present, it is the clinicians who have the responsibility of deciding what should happen in the best interests of a mentally incapacitated adult.

While most relatives would wish to act in the best interests of the mentally incapacitated adult, one cannot be certain whether June falls in the minority who are only thinking of themselves. For example, if

June said, 'Do not operate. My father has had a good life. Let him die,' it may be that her decision was because she was overwhelmed with debt and had a huge mortgage and was only thinking that, as the sole beneficiary, she would inherit all her father's estate. In the Department of Health's *Guidance on Consent to Examination or Treatment* (2001a), form 4 covers the situation where an adult is incapable of giving a valid consent because of mental disorder. Form 4 is not properly a 'consent form' since it records an absence of consent. The health practitioner recommending that treatment is in the best interests of a mentally incapable adult, must record the fact of and the reason for the mental incapacity, enable the relatives to record their knowledge of the situation and the fact that the proposed treatment is in the patient's best interests (note that the relatives do not give consent, because they have no legal power to do that), and a second health practitioner can also sign the form if the treatment is to be performed by another person. Where nurses become aware that relatives are being asked to give consent for a mentally incapacitated adult, they should draw the attention of the health practitioner concerned to this form and the Department of Health forms and guidance.

Conclusions

The present situation is clearly unsatisfactory. Statutory provision is urgently required so that mentally incapable adults can be protected. In many ways the present situation is a denial of their rights as set out in the European Convention on Human Rights, which came into force in England and Wales following the implementation of the Human Rights Act on 2 October 2000 (*Chapter 1*). (The Act came into force in Scotland on devolution.)

A new Mental Health Act is proposed (DoH, 2000; DoH, 2002) which will provide greater protection for mentally incapacitated adults. In addition there will be legislation which will implement the

Government's proposals for decision making on their behalf.

At present, health professionals (except those in Scotland — see above) have to rely on common law powers to act in the best interests of the mentally incapacitated adult, and know when it is advisable to seek a declaration of the courts. In the meantime, to assist health professionals, patients, relatives, lawyers and others (since in the words of the consultation paper 'new legislation' takes time) the Lord Chancellor has initiated a consultation paper on several leaflets which are to be issued to different groups who are involved in decision making by people who have difficulty deciding for themselves (Lord Chancellor's Department Consultation Paper, 2002). The consultation ended on 9 July 2002 and it is hoped that these leaflets will provide some interim assistance in a difficult area. Provision is included in the draft Mental Health Bill (*Chapter 25*) for the protection of informal (ie. not detained) patients who are incapable of giving consent but do not resist treatment (ie. compliant incapacitated patients). Part 5 of the draft bill (Clauses 121–139) seeks to provide safeguards for such patients and ensure compliance with Article 5 of the European Convention of Human Rights. Such patients can still be treated informally under the common law, but the safeguards should protect them against inappropriate treatment or detention. Informal patients who resist proposed treatment and are at a substantial risk of committing suicide or causing serious harm to others can only be given treatment using the compulsory powers available under Part 5 and 2 of the bill. At the time of writing a consultation exercise on the draft bill is taking place and it is unlikely that legislation will be in force before the end of 2003. In the meantime, the Mental Health Act 1983 and common law powers must be used, but it would be wise for health professionals to ensure that as far as possible the rights of the patient under the European Convention of Human Rights are respected.

References

Bolam v. *Friern Hospital Management Committee* [1957] 1 WLR 582

Department of Health (2000) White Paper: *Reforming the Mental Health Act*. Cm 5016–1. The Stationery Office, London

Department of Health (2001a) *Reference guide on consent to examination or treatment*. DoH, London

Department of Health (2001b) *Good practice in consent implementation guide*. DoH, London

Department of Health (2002) *Draft Mental Health Bill* (issued for consultation)

Law Commission (1995) *Mental Incapacity*. Report No 231. HMSO, London

Lord Chancellor's Department Consultation Paper (2002) *Making Decisions: Helping People who have Difficulty Deciding for Themselves.* Online at: http://www.lcd.gov.uk/consult/family/decision.htm

Lord Chancellor's Office (1997) *Who Decides? Decision making on behalf of the mentally incapacitated adult*. The Stationery Office, London

Lord Chancellor's Office (1999) *Making Decisions: The Government's proposals for decision making on behalf of the mentally incapacitated adult*. The Stationery Office, London

Re F. (mental patient: sterilisation) [1990] 2 AC 1

8

Young persons of sixteen and seventeen years

> **Box 8.1: Case scenario**
>
> A sixteen-year-old girl under local authority care was suffering from anorexia nervosa. At one point she was fed by nasogastric tube and had her arms encased in plaster. Her condition became critical and she refused to move to a specialist hospital. The local authority applied to the High Court for the girl to be transferred to a treatment unit without her consent, and for leave to give her medical treatment without her consent. Leave was given by the High Court judge. By 30 June, although five feet, seven inches tall, she weighed only five stone, seven pounds. The Court of Appeal made an emergency order enabling her to be taken to and treated at a specialist hospital in London, notwithstanding her lack of consent (*Re W. (a minor) (medical treatment)* [1992]).

Introduction

It is only recently that the rights of children and young persons have been given weight; some would argue that they are still treated with excessive paternalism. The British Medical Association (BMA) has advocated that greater information should be given to the child and young person and that they should have greater involvement in their own care, treatment and decision making (BMA, 2001). This chapter looks at the law relating to young persons of sixteen and seventeen years.

Statutory right to give consent

A young person of sixteen and seventeen years has a statutory right to give consent under Section 8(1) of the Family Law Reform Act 1969:

> *The consent of a minor who has attained the age of sixteen years, to any surgical, medical or dental treatment, which in the absence of consent, would constitute a trespass to the person, shall be as effective as it would be if he were of full age; and where a minor has by virtue of this section given an effective consent to any treatment it shall not be necessary to obtain any consent for it from his parent or guardian.*

Section 8(1) makes it clear that the consent of the young person is effective in its own right; consent does not also have to be obtained from the parent or guardian. There is in law a presumption that a sixteen- or seventeen-year-old has the necessary capacity, but this can be rebutted if there is evidence to the contrary, as, for example, in the case of a sixteen-year-old with learning difficulties.

Consent to what?

Section 8(2) explains:

> *... the section 'surgical, medical or dental treatment' includes any procedure undertaken for the purposes of diagnosis and this section applies to any procedures (including, in particular, the administration of an anaesthetic) which is ancillary to any treatment as it applies to that treatment.*

This is a comprehensive definition and covers most care and treatment provided in hospital and the community by all health professionals. It does not specifically refer to complementary or alternative therapies but if these are provided under the aegis of a registered health professional there is no reason why the young person could not give a valid consent for them. It does not cover consent to research, which would be in a different category, unless the research was part of the young person's treatment (see *Chapter 21*).

Parental consent and the young person

Section 8(3) makes it clear that the fact that a young person of sixteen and seventeen years now has a statutory right to give consent does not invalidate any other consent, which would have been valid before 1969.

> *Nothing in the section shall be construed as making ineffective any consent which would have been effective if this section had not been enacted.*

In other words, before 1969, a parent or guardian could give consent on behalf of a child and young person until he/she became an adult (ie. twenty-one years before the 1969 Act, eighteen years after the 1969 Act). This power of the parent or guardian to give consent still continues and a health professional can rely on the consent of either the young person or his or her parent as a defence against an action for trespass to the person. For example, if a young man of seventeen was brought unconscious into hospital following a road accident, the parents could give consent to any necessary treatment on his behalf. The health professionals could also act in the best interests of the unconscious person (*Chapters 7* and *11*).

Overruling a child's consent to treatment

In a situation such as a termination of a pregnancy, the young person of sixteen or seventeen years may give consent for the termination, but there have been cases where the parents have attempted to prevent the termination taking place on the grounds that they would look after the child. In such a situation, the health professionals could act on the valid basis of the young person's statutory right to give consent and the parents' attempt to prevent the termination going ahead would fail. Such a dispute arose in the case of a girl of fifteen years who had had a previous pregnancy and the judge refused to prevent the termination going ahead on the grounds that it was in her best interests (*Re P. (a minor)* (1981)).

There may be other circumstances where the treatment required by the young person was not in his/her best interests. For example, the young person might seek to be sterilised. In such circumstances, the parents could seek to make the child a ward of court or invoke the court's inherent jurisdiction for the matter to be brought before the courts. The older the child, the less likely the court is to interfere with the child's wishes.

Refusal to consent by a young person

In the case of *Re W.* (*Box 8.1, p. 66*) the Court of Appeal held that the Family Law Reform Act 1969 section 8 did not prevent consent being given by parents or the court. While the girl had a right to give consent under the Act, she could not refuse treatment which was necessary to save her life. Her refusal was therefore overruled.

The courts would not lightly overrule the refusal of a young person. There would have to be strong evidence that it was a life-saving matter. There is a clear difference between a parent acting on behalf of a mentally incapacitated young person in his/her best interests and a parent wishing to overrule the explicit wishes of a youngster. In the latter case, referral to the courts under the Children Act 1989 or under its inherent jurisdiction to consider cases involving children would be necessary. If parents disagree over the action which should be taken in relation to a young person of sixteen or seventeen years, the case can be brought to court under the Children Act 1989. Where possible, the court would wish to give effect to the wishes of a mentally capacitated child.

As a result of the decision in *Re W.* and other cases and the view that in a life-saving situation the refusal of a young person could be overruled by the court, it is clear that young persons of sixteen and seventeen years are not treated as adults and do not have the same rights that a mentally competent adult would have to refuse life-saving treatment. It has been suggested that competence is defined more strictly in the case of young people than in the case of adults to protect them from the worst effects of their decision (BMA, 2001). In other words, a certain paternalism lawfully exists in relation to decision making by and on behalf of young people. As yet there has not been a case where a young person has challenged such an attitude under the Human Rights Act 1998, arguing that Article 3 (the right not to be subjected to inhuman or degrading treatment or punishment) is infringed when a young person's wishes are overruled. For example, if instead of suffering from anorexia nervosa, the girl in the case scenario was suffering from leukaemia and required a blood transfusion as a life-saving necessity, but was refusing a blood transfusion because she was a Jehovah's Witness, would the courts take the same view as it did in *Re W.* and overrule her refusal? At eighteen years a refusal by a mentally competent adult in such circumstances would not be overruled, but the situation for the sixteen- and seventeen-year-old still has to be clarified by the courts. The present situation could be seen as contrary to the young person's rights under Article 3 and Article 9 (freedom of religious expression).

Consent to research

While the Family Law Reform Act 1969 does not give a statutory right to the young person to give consent to research which is not part of a treatment plan, it is thought that there would be a right at common law (judge-made or case law) for a young person who had the mental capacity to give a valid consent. This would be a consequence of the House of Lords ruling in the Gillick case (*Gillick* v. *W. Norfolk and Wisbech Area Health Authority* [1986]) which is considered in the next chapter.

Conclusion

It is likely that we shall see more cases involving children and young persons where their rights under the European Convention on Human Rights are urged. Young persons of sixteen and seventeen are not in law adults, but those who care for them should be able to justify (and document) decisions taken on their behalf. The next chapter considers the law relating to the child under sixteen years.

References

British Medical Association (2001) *Consent, Rights and Choices in Health Care for Children and Young People.* BMJ Books, London

Gillick v. *W. Norfolk and Wisbech Area Health Authority* [1986] 1 AC 112

Re P. (a minor) (1981) 80 LGR 301

Re W. (a minor) (medical treatment) [1992] 4 All ER 627

9

Children under the age of sixteen years

Box 9.1: Case scenario

Mrs Gillick questioned the lawfulness of the Department of Health and Social Security (DHSS) circular HN[80]46, which was a revised version of part of a comprehensive memorandum of guidance on family planning services issued to health authorities in May 1974 under cover of circular HSC(IS)32. The circular stated that in certain circumstances a doctor could lawfully prescribe contraception for a girl under sixteen without the consent of the parents. Mrs Gillick wrote to the acting administrator formally forbidding any medical staff employed by the Norfolk Area Health Authority (AHA) to give, 'any contraceptive or abortion advice or treatment whatever to my... daughters whilst they are under sixteen years without my consent.'

The administrator replied that the treatment prescribed by a doctor is a matter for the doctor's clinical judgement, taking into account all the factors of the case. Mrs Gillick, who had five daughters, brought an action against the AHA and the DHSS seeking a declaration that the notice gave advice which was unlawful and wrong and which did or might adversely affect the welfare of her children, her right as a parent and her ability to discharge properly her duties as a parent. She sought a declaration that no doctor or other professional person employed by the health authority might give any contraceptive or abortion advice or treatment to any of her children below the age of sixteen without her previous knowledge and consent.

Source: *Gillick v. West Norfolk and Wisbeck AHA and the DHSS* [1985]

Introduction

In the last chapter it was explained that there was a statutory right for a young person of sixteen and seventeen years to give consent to treatment. There is no such statutory right for those under sixteen and the law there has been laid down by the courts (common law or judge-made law). The leading case is that of Mrs Gillick, the facts of which are set out in *Box 9.1*.

Mrs Gillick had, it seemed, a strong case. Under the Family Law Reform Act 1969, section 8(1), a young person of sixteen or seventeen had a statutory right to give consent, so it could be concluded that a child under sixteen lacked the power in law to give consent to treatment.

Although Mrs Gillick lost the case in the High Court, her appeal to the Court of Appeal succeeded, where all three judges unanimously agreed with her and also held that a doctor who gave contraceptive advice to an underage girl would be aiding and abetting in a criminal offence, since it was unlawful for a man to have intercourse with a girl under sixteen years.

The Department of Health appealed to the House of Lords, where there was a majority decision in upholding the appeal and reversing the decision of the Court of Appeal.

Narrow interpretation of the House of Lords' decision

On the narrow view, the House of Lords held that in exceptional circumstances a girl under sixteen could give consent to contraceptive advice and treatment without parental consent. The exceptional circumstances listed by Lord Fraser were that:

❖ The girl would, although under sixteen, understand the doctor's advice.

❖ The doctor could not persuade her to inform her parents or allow him/her to inform the parents that she was seeking contraceptive advice.

❖ She was very likely to have sexual intercourse with or without contraceptive treatment.

❖ Unless she received contraceptive advice or treatment her physical and/or mental health were likely to suffer.

❖ Her best interests required him to give her contraceptive advice, treatment, or both, without parental consent.

Wider interpretation of the House of Lords' decision

On a wider interpretation, the House of Lords held that a Gillick-competent (see below) boy or girl could give a valid consent to treatment which was in his/her best interests without the involvement of parents.

The Gillick-competent child

The expression 'the Gillick-competent' child has now come into regular use. It refers to a child of any age who has achieved sufficient understanding and intelligence to enable him/her to understand fully what is proposed. The level of understanding must, of course, relate to the nature of the decision to be made (*Box 9.2*).

Box 9.2: Fictional case: child in need of simple treatment

John, a boy of ten years, came into the accident and emergency department accompanied by his friend of the same age. They had been playing on a refuse dump and John had fallen against some broken glass and suffered a long cut to his leg. It was bleeding profusely. John said that his parents were at work and it appeared that the boys were playing truant from school. The nurse explained to John that he would have to have stitches in his leg. He understood what she was saying and appeared to give a valid consent. What is the law?

In the fictional situation in *Box 9.2*, it is possible that John is Gillick-competent, that he is capable of understanding what is involved in the treatment and could give a valid consent. Contact should be attempted with his parents, but in the meantime treatment could proceed on the basis of the consent given by John.

In addition, if it were felt that John were not Gillick-competent, emergency treatment could be given to him under the common law power to act out of necessity, recognised in the case of *Re F. (mental patient: sterilisation)* [1990] (*Chapter 7*).

In this situation, the health professionals also have power, under the Children Act 1989, to act in the interests of the child, as section 3(5) shows:

A person who (a) does not have parental responsibility for a particular child, but (b) has care of the child, may (subject to the provision of this Act) do what is reasonable in all the circumstances of the case for the purpose of safeguarding or promoting the child's welfare.

This would appear to include giving consent to necessary emergency treatment in the absence of the parents as in the above situation.

If, in contrast to some stitches in his leg, John needed brain surgery or some other dangerous and risky procedure, he would probably not be seen as Gillick-competent and health professionals would not act on the basis of his consent alone. They would still have a duty to ensure that any emergency action was taken to save the child's life, if parental consent could not be obtained in time.

Health professionals often find that children who suffer from chronic conditions and who receive regular hospitalisation develop a maturity above their physical years and an understanding of the proposed treatment. They should be given as much information as is reasonable to develop their understanding as shown in *Box 9.3* .

Box 9.3: Refusal of treatment

Jayne suffered from cystic fibrosis and her condition had deteriorated over recent years. She was now on oxygen for most of the day and night and took additional feeding through a gastrostomy tube. She was fourteen years and had been placed on a waiting list for a lung transplant. Her condition progressively deteriorated and she started rejecting the regular physiotherapy. It was explained that physiotherapy was vital to keep her as well as possible for such time as a lung transplant was available. However, she said that she did not believe that a transplant was the answer and she wanted to be allowed to die. Her parents wanted all efforts to be made for her to be kept alive because of the possibility of donor organs becoming available. What is the law?

Crucial to the answer to the tragic circumstances in *Box 9.3* is the mental capacity of Jayne. She probably has a very good understanding of her condition, and realises that many people on the waiting list for a transplant die before they have the operation. She may have formed a realistic view of her situation and her wish to die may be a wish formed by a Gillick-competent person, in which case it could be respected in law.

In contrast, her parents want active treatment to proceed. In this dilemma, much will depend on the realities of the clinical situation. If doctors assess Jayne's chances as slim, and active intervention as not only very uncomfortable but also futile, they may support Jayne's decision as being reasonable under the circumstances. It may be that, realistically, Jayne would be too ill to have a transplant. (The legal issues raised by the right to die are discussed in another book by the same author, *Legal Aspects of Pain Management*.) This is a different situation from the facts of the case shown in *Box 9.4*.

Box 9.4: Refusing a transplant (*Re M. (medical treatment: consent)* [1999])

A girl of fifteen years refused to consent to a transplant which was needed to save her life. She stated that she did not wish to have anyone else's heart and she did not wish to take medication for the rest of her life. The hospital, which had obtained her mother's consent to the transplant, sought leave from the court to carry out the transplant. The girl was an intelligent person whose wishes carried considerable weight, but she had been overwhelmed by her circumstances and the decision she was being asked to make. Her severe condition had developed only recently and she had had only a few days to consider her situation. While recognising the risk that for the rest of her life she would carry resentment about what had been done to her, the court weighed that risk against the certainty of death if the order were not made.

The difference between the situations in *Box 9.3* and *Box 9.4* is clear. In Jayne's case she had lived with cystic fibrosis all her life and was aware of her own situation and the fact that she may not survive for a transplant. In the case shown in *Box 9.4*, the girl was afflicted suddenly with a heart condition and could not adjust easily to her new situation.

In the next chapter, we will consider the case where both the patient, a boy of fifteen, and his parents, were Jehovah's Witnesses and both the parents' and the boy's refusal to consent to a blood transfusion were overruled.

Parental rights

In addition to the right of the Gillick-competent child to give consent to necessary treatment, the parents also have the right to give consent. However, their rights must be exercised in the best interests of the child. There are examples where the parents' refusal to arrange for the necessary treatment has been overruled, and there are examples where treatment arranged by the parents has been stopped as not being in the child's best interests. In every case, the paramount consideration is the welfare of the child. This will be considered further in the next chapter. All the principles about information giving which are discussed in *Chapters 4* and 5 apply to ensuring that parents have the necessary information about the care and treatment of their children. The Kennedy report (2001) recommended that:

> *(Recommendation 15). Parents of those too young to take decisions for themselves should receive a copy of any letter written by one healthcare professional to another about their child's treatment or care.*

Evidence that consent has been given

The forms set out in the *Good practice in consent implementation guide: consent to examination or treatment* (DoH, 2001) can be used as evidence that consent has been given by the parent or child (where competent) or both. Form 2 is used by a child and parent of a child, where it is anticipated that the child will lose consciousness, and form 3 for treatment where the patient will remain conscious. In practice, some trusts are finding that form 2 is suitable for all procedures to be carried out on children.

Conclusion

Acting in the best interests of the child and enabling the child to have as much input into critical decisions can be seen as a considerable challenge to health professionals, who are not helped by disputes between separated or divorced parents.

It is important to ensure that even in the case of very young children, the child is involved in the decisions relating to his/her care, given as much information as is reasonable for his/her level of understanding and his/her autonomy promoted as fully as possible.

In the next chapter we will consider the law relating to disputes between parents and between parents and professionals.

References

Department of Health (2001) *Good practice in consent implementation guide: consent to examination or treatment.* DoH, London: November

Dimond B (2002) *Legal Aspects of Pain Management.* Quay Books, Mark Allen Publishing Limited, Salisbury, Wiltshire

Gillick v. *West Norfolk and Wisbech AHA and the DHSS* [1985] 3 All ER 402

Re F. (mental patient: sterilisation) [1990] 2 AC 1

Kennedy I (2001) Bristol Royal Infirmary Inquiry Learning from Bristol: the report of the public inquiry into children's heart surgery at the Bristol Royal Infirmary 1984–1995. Command paper CM 5207. Stationery Office, London

Re M. (medical treatment: consent) [1999] 2FLR 1097

10

Disputes with parents

Box 10.1: Case scenario

David has been separated from his wife Julie for several years. Their six-year-old son, Jonathan, is in hospital and doctors have advised that he needs a tonsillectomy. David has said that he is not prepared to give consent to such an operation because he had a similar operation when he was eight years old and believed that it was carried out simply because tonsillectomies were fashionable at the time. Julie wants the operation to proceed and is prepared to sign the consent form. What is the law?

Introduction

The last chapter considered the law relating to consent by a child under sixteen years, noting that a parent could give consent on behalf of the child but in certain circumstances, the child, if Gillick-competent, could give consent on his/her own behalf. This chapter considers the situation where there are disputes with parents over what is in the child's best interests.

Box 10.2: Case of *Re E. (a minor) (wardship: medical treatment)* [1993]

A youth of fifteen years nine months suffering from leukaemia required a blood transfusion as part of his treatment. Both he and his parents were Jehovah's Witnesses and refused to give consent. The health authority applied for him to be made a ward of court and for a declaration that the treatment could proceed. The judge held that the lad was intelligent enough to take decisions about his own well-being, but that he did not have a full understanding of what the blood transfusions would involve. The welfare of the child was the first and paramount consideration. Although the court should be very slow to interfere in a decision the child had taken, the welfare of the child led to only one conclusion: that the hospital should be at liberty to treat him with blood transfusions. The judge gave leave to the hospital authority to give treatment, including blood transfusion, and the consent of the patient and his parents was dispensed with.

Parental rights

Parental refusal overruled

In the case in *Box 10.2*, the parents had pleaded that the boy's refusal should be upheld because he would have been sixteen years in only a few months time. However, as discussed in *Chapter 8*, the case of *Re W. (a minor) (medical treatment)* [1992] shows it is not until a person with the requisite mental capacity is eighteen years that his/her refusal to have life-saving treatment is protected.

A case similar to that in *Box 10.2* was that of Re S. (*Re S. (a minor) (consent to medical treatment)* [1994]). A girl of fifteen years suffered from thalassaemia and had been kept alive by monthly blood transfusions and injections. She and her mother became Jehovah's

Witnesses and subsequently refused to accept blood transfusions. The judge decided that the treatment could be authorised on the grounds that it was in her best interests and the court had the power to overrule a competent child's refusal of treatment. He did, however, find that the girl was not Gillick-competent because she lacked emotional maturity.

In the case of *Re S. (a minor)(medical treatment)* [1993] the child was four and a half years and suffering from T-cell leukaemia. It appeared that the only clinical option for her survival was a blood transfusion as part of the treatment, but her parents who were Jehovah's Witnesses refused to give consent to this aspect of her care. The local authority sought leave of the court to invoke the inherent jurisdiction of the court under Section 100 of the Children Act 1989 and for a declaration that a blood transfusion could be given. The judge agreed to the declaration and considered that fears that in the future the child would believe her life to have been perpetuated by an ungodly act to have little foundation in reality. The judge stated that, 'the reality seems to me to be that family reaction which recognise that the responsibility for consent was taken from them and, as a judicial act, absolved their conscience of responsibility.'

Failure by parents to arrange for the necessary treatment to be provided for their children can, in certain circumstances, and where the child dies, constitute the crime of murder or manslaughter. A father was imprisoned and the mother was given a suspended sentence when they treated their diabetic daughter with a herbal remedy, rather than arrange for her to have insulin (*The Times*, 1993).

Refusal of screening

In the case of *Re C. (HIV test)* [1999], a mother was HIV positive but the parents refused to have her four-month-old baby tested for HIV. The local authority applied for a specific issue order that the baby be tested. The Court of Appeal upheld the judge's order that it was in the best interests of the child to be tested for HIV. There was no order that breast feeding of the baby should be discontinued in the event of the child being found negative. The trial judge believed that such an order (which had not been sought) would be unenforceable. The Human Rights Act 1998 had not been brought into force at the time the case was decided and it could be argued that to compel the baby to be tested was a breach of Article 8 and the right to respect for privacy and family life. However, if the test was considered to be in the best interests of the baby, then this could come under one of the exceptions to Article 8 (see the *Appendix).*

The general principle is that if the parents are refusing to give consent to life-saving treatment, which doctors consider is necessary in the best interests of the child, then the court can intervene and declare that it is lawful to proceed without the consent of the parents. In an emergency situation, where there is insufficient time to obtain a declaration from the courts (and there is an on-call system, so a decision can be obtained speedily), doctors would be justified in law in acting in the best interests of the child and in carrying out life-saving treatment.

In such a situation, they could obtain a retrospective declaration from the courts that they acted in the child's best interests. In other words, a child should not be allowed to die because parental consent to the treatment is lacking. There is also a power under the Children Act 1989 section 3(5) (*Chapter 9*) which enables the carer of the child, 'to do what is reasonable in all the circumstances of the case for the purpose of safeguarding or promoting the child's welfare'.

> **Box 10.3:** *Re D. (a minor) (wardship: sterilisation)* **[1976]**
>
> A girl of eleven years suffered from Sotos' syndrome, the symptoms of which include accelerated growth during infancy, epilepsy, general clumsiness, an unusual facial appearance and behaviour problems, including emotional instability, certain aggressive tendencies and some impairment of mental function. The mother, taking the advice of the consultant paediatrician that her daughter would remain substantially handicapped and that she would always be unable to care for herself or look after any children, discussed with the obstetrician the possibility of her daughter being sterilised. An operation was arranged. However, before it was performed the educational psychologist applied for the girl to be made a ward of court. Mrs Justice Heilbron, who heard the case, was not convinced that the operation was in the best interests of the girl and so ordered that the operation should not proceed.

Case where parents' refusal upheld

In general, it is unusual for the courts not to uphold the medical view of what is in the best interests of the child. In the case shown in *Box 10. 4* the Court of Appeal supported the parents' refusal to allow their child to have a liver transplant. This was an unusual decision, and specific to the atypical facts of the case.

> **Box 10.4: *Re T. (a minor) (wardship: medical treatment)* [1996]**
>
> The child was in need of a liver transplant but parents refused to give permission for the operation to take place. Medical opinion was that the child would have a reasonable chance of success from such an operation. However, the parents were living abroad and would have to bring the child to the UK for the operation to take place. The High Court held that leave should be given for the health professionals to perform the operation despite parental opposition. The Court of Appeal overruled this ruling and placed emphasis on the views of the parents and the fact that they were both health professionals. It decided that it was not in the child's best interests for it to order the child to return to the UK for the transplant operation to take place.

When treatment wanted by parents is stopped

Following the case described in *Box 10.3*, the judge recommended that such cases of non-therapeutic sterilisations should be brought before the courts for a declaration to be made that they were in the child's best interests. Such cases are unusual, since normally treatment agreed between parents and doctors for a child would be considered to be in the child's best interests. However, the case is a precedent for any person who is concerned at the treatment which is proposed for the child. An application can be made to make the child a ward of court or, under the Children Act 1989, for a declaration to be made as to what is in the child's best interests.

Disputes between parents over the child's treatment

Even when parents are divorced or separated, under the Children Act 1989 section 2(1) both parents retain parental responsibility for their children. Under section 2(7) where more than one person has parental responsibility for a child, each of them may act alone and without the other (or others) in meeting that responsibility. Even where one parent has a residence order in his/her favour, the other still retains parental responsibilities and can exercise these to the full. It also follows that one parent does not have the right of veto over the other's actions.

If, however, there has been a specific order by the court relating to a decision affecting the care or treatment of the child, then a single parent cannot change this or take any action which is incompatible with this order unless the approval of the court is obtained. It follows that if there is a dispute between parents over treatment decisions in respect of the child, either can go to court for a specific issue or prohibited steps order to be made.

Prohibited steps order

Where one parent wishes to prevent the other taking action which he/she does not consider is in the interests of the child, he/she may seek a prohibited steps order. This can be ordered under section 8 of the Children Act 1989, which means that no step which could be taken by a parent in meeting his/her parental responsibility for a child and which is of a kind specified in the order shall be taken without the consent of the court. Thus, if one parent feared that the other was likely to agree to a mentally impaired daughter being sterilised, then that parent could obtain a prohibited steps order preventing the operation proceeding on the basis of consent by the other parent, unless the court were to so direct.

If the child is considered to be Gillick-competent but disagrees with actions which the parents are intending, he/she could seek the leave of the court to obtain a prohibited steps order. The child would have to apply to the High Court (*Re D. (a minor) (wardship: sterilisation)* [1976]). The court must be satisfied that the child has sufficient understanding to make the proposed application (section 10(8) of the Children Act 1989).

Unmarried parents

Under present law, an unmarried father can acquire parental responsibilities by court order or agreement with the mother. If he marries the mother he acquires it automatically through the legitimation of the child. Under amendments made by the Adoption and Children Act 2002, he will be able to acquire it automatically on being registered as the father. Because health professionals may not always be aware of the marital status of the parents, they may have to assume that only the mother has parental responsibilities unless there is clear evidence to the contrary.

Case scenario

With regard to the 'case scenario' (*Box 10.1*), the father is entitled to apply under the Children Act 1989 for the case to be heard on whether the operation is in the child's best interests, and whether a prohibited steps order should be made. Evidence would be brought before the court of expert views of Jonathan's clinical condition and whether reasonable practice (*Bolam* v. *Friern Hospital Management Committee QBD* [1957]) would justify the operation. In the light of this evidence the judge would make his order.

Conclusion

As more marriages and relationships break down and new partnerships are formed, health practitioners on children's wards will find that they become involved in conflicts between the parties, where the child's treatment is used as an object of conflict. Health professionals should be familiar with the process for resolving any such major dilemma over what action should be taken in the best interests of the child. Where a major conflict is anticipated, it is preferable to seek the declaration of the court, earlier rather than later, since this enables all parties, including the child, to be represented. Health practitioners must, as always, ensure that their documentation, which is likely to be produced in court, is of the highest standard.

References

Bolam v. *Friern Hospital Management Committee QBD* [1957] 2 All ER 118

Re C. (HIV test) [1999] 2 FLR 1004

Re D. (a minor) (wardship: sterilisation) [1976] 1 All ER 327

Re E. (a minor) (wardship: medical treatment) [1993] 1 FLR 386

Re S. (a minor) (medical treatment) [1993] 1 FLR 376

Re S. (a minor) (consent to medical treatment) [1994] 2 FLR 1065

Re T. (a minor) (wardship: medical treatment) [1996] *The Times*, 28 October 1996; [1997] 1 WLR 242.

Re W. (a minor) (medical treatment) [1992] 4 All ER 627

The Times (1993) News report. The Times, 29 October

11

Determining 'best interests'

Box 11.1: Case scenario

The claimant, aged thirty-six years, sought a declaration from the court that two preliminary blood tests and a conventional bone marrow harvesting operation under general anaesthetic could be lawfully taken from and performed upon her sister Y. The facts were that the applicant was suffering from a pre-leukaemic bone marrow disorder. She had undergone extensive chemotherapy and a blood stem cell transplant. She had started to deteriorate and was likely to progress to acute myeloid leukaemia over the next three months. Her only realistic prospect of recovery was a bone marrow transplant operation from a healthy compatible donor. Preliminary investigations suggested that Y., her sister, would be a suitable donor. Y. was twenty-five years and severely mentally and physically handicapped. She had lived in a community home for eight years. She was incapable of giving consent to the donation of bone marrow. The court had to decide whether it was in the best interests of Y. for a declaration to be made for the blood tests and the bone marrow harvesting to take place (*Re Y. (adult patient) (transplant: bone marrow)* [1997]).

Introduction

Where an adult lacks the mental capacity to make his/her own decisions, then in the absence of any statutory provision, health professionals have a power, recognised at common law, to act in the best interests of that person (*Re F. (mental patient: sterilisation)* [1990]; see *Chapter 7*). This chapter explores what is meant by 'best interests' and whether the situation in the above case scenario could come within such a definition.

Determining best interests

Law Commission proposals

In 1995, after an extensive consultation exercise, the Law Commission (1995) published its proposals for setting up a framework for decisions to be made on behalf of mentally incapacitated adults. This document suggests how 'best interests' can be determined (*Table 11.1*).

Table 11.1: How to determine a person's best interests
In deciding what is in a person's best interests regard should be had to:

1. The ascertainable past and present wishes and feelings of the person concerned, and the factors that person would consider if able to do so

2. The need to permit and encourage the person to participate, or to improve his/her ability to participate, as fully as possible, in anything done for and any decision affecting him/her

3. The views of other people whom it is appropriate and practicable to consult about the person's wishes and feelings and what would be in his/her best interests

4. Whether the purpose for which any action or decision is required can be as effectively achieved in a manner less restrictive of the person's freedom of action

Source: Law Commission (1995)

Substituted judgement

There is a difference between making decisions on behalf of a person who once had mental capacity and has now lost it, and a person who has always lacked the mental capacity to make decisions. For example, a person who is a Jehovah's Witness might become a victim of Alzheimer's disease and a situation may arise where that person requires a blood transfusion. Using the Law Commission's definition (*Table 11.1*), 'the ascertainable past wishes and feelings of that person, and the factors that person would consider if able to do so' would indicate that the person would not wish to have a blood transfusion. In applying the best interest test the wish not to receive blood would be respected. In this sense, it is a modified best interests test, since simply applying best interests, ie. to keep alive, would have indicated that the blood transfusion should be given.

What one is applying here is a substituted judgement test: what would this person want if he could now speak his mind? In contrast, a person suffering from severe learning disabilities may never have acquired the capacity to make decisions, so best interests must simply relate to his/her present situation and what would be seen as reasonable care. In this sense the question is: would the procedure envisaged benefit the patient?

In the leading case of *Re F. (mental patient: sterilisation)* [1990] (*Chapter 7*), where the sterilisation of a woman with severe learning disabilities was in issue, the court held that it was to her benefit that she had the operation, since she had formed a sexual relationship with another patient and she could not have understood the pregnancy or coped with the birth and bringing up a child.

Critics of the decision could argue that sterilisation might prevent a pregnancy, but it may not have been in her best interests since she would be vulnerable to abuse, exploitation, venereal diseases, etc. and if she received the care appropriate to a mental age of five she would not have been in the situation where she could become pregnant. The Supreme Court of Canada took a different decision to the House of Lords on very similar facts (Re Eve, 1986).

Altruism and best interests

The substituted judgement test allows for altruistic decisions to be made. Under this test, as opposed to the simple best interests test, a decision which benefits other people could be made on behalf of the mentally incapacitated adult.

Distinction between temporary and permanent or semi-permanent incapacity

This distinction is important in determining what is in someone's best interests. If the incapacity is only temporary, eg. in the case of a person unconscious after a road accident, only limited decision making is required. Treatment must be given until capacity is restored and then the person can take his/her own decisions. In contrast, where a person is unlikely to recover his/her mental capacity, as in the case of a person with Alzheimer's disease or with learning disabilities, decisions of a non-urgent kind have to be made on a day-to-day basis.

Best interests and risk assessment

Health professionals who care for those who, temporarily or permanently, are unable to make their own decisions, need to include within their treatment plans a consideration of action necessary in the patient's best interests and be aware of how this could be justified in the event of its being challenged. Those caring for patients with learning disabilities may, for example, decide that taking part in a day trip is in the best interests of a particular patient, and reasonably foreseeable risks are identified and action taken to minimise or remove them altogether. Consent form 4 of the Department of Health's practical guidance on consent (DoH, 2001), which is considered in *Chapter 7*, requires the health professional who is caring for a mentally competent adult to identify the treatment which is to be given and to give reasons why it is in the patient's best interests.

In certain circumstances, best interests may justify some form of restraint. However, this should only be on a temporary basis and the justification clearly identified. Any longer-term restraint should be within the provisions of mental health legislation. The fourth point of the Law Commission's definition should be applied (*Table 11.1*). (The Government has published a White paper, but legislation is still awaited; Lord Chancellor, 1999.)

Case scenario

What decision did the court make in the case of Re Y.? In the first case, the judge made it clear that it was the best interests of Y. which were in dispute. The best interests of the sister were not relevant, save in so far as they served the best interests of Y.

The judge argued as follows: if the sister did not have the bone marrow transplant she would die. This would be a devastating blow to her mother, who suffered from ill health. They were a very close family. The mother would find it more difficult to visit Y. in the community home, especially as after the death of Y.'s sister, she would then have to look after her only grandchild. Y. would suffer as a result of the lack of contact with her mother. The risk of harm to Y. from the blood tests was negligible. Although a general anaesthetic posed some risk, it was a low risk. She had already had a general anaesthetic for a hysterectomy without any apparent adverse ill effects. The bone marrow would regenerate. It was to Y.'s emotional, psychological and social benefit for her to be a donor. It would, therefore, be in the best interests of Y. for her to have the blood tests and be a donor for her sister.

Conclusions

There are considerable dangers that the case of Y. could start a slippery slope. If bone marrow is justified, why not a kidney? It would be morally unacceptable for our community homes for those with learning disabilities to be seen as the source of spare parts and organ donations. Yet, in an American case, decided before Re Y., it was held that a mentally handicapped patient could be a live kidney donor for his brother (*Strunk* v. *Strunk*, 1996). Statutory provision for making decisions on behalf of mentally incapacitated adults, together with a statutory definition of best interests on the line suggested by the Law Commission, is essential to ensure that the human rights of mentally incapacitated adults are protected.

References

Department of Health (2001) *Good practice in consent implementation guide: consent to examination or treatment*. DoH, London: November

Law Commission (1995) *Mental Incapacity*. Report No. 231. HMSO, London

Lord Chancellor (1999) *Making Decisions on Behalf of Mentally Incapacitated Adults*. Lord Chancellor's Office, London

Re Eve (1986) 31 DLR (4th) 1 (Can SC)

Re F. (mental patient: sterilisation) [1990] 2 AC 1

Re Y. (adult patient) (transplant: bone marrow) [1997] 2 WLR 556

Strunk v. *Strunk* (1996) 445 SW 2d 145 (Ky CA)

se decisions, which received adverse publicity, there was a
cation by the Court of Appeal and this came in the case of

MB.

f MB. (*Box 12.1*), the judge held that the woman was
apacitated as a result of the phobia and the operation
re proceed in her best interests. The same day the Court
held that decision. In a reserved judgement it set out how
to be determined (*Table 12.1*) and the general principles
to the refusal of treatment (*Table 12.2*).

Determining capacity: Re MB.

ks the capacity if some impairment or disturbance of mental
renders the person unable to make a decision whether to
r to refuse treatment. That inability to make a decision will

tient is unable to comprehend and retain the information which
erial to the decision, especially as to the likely consequences of
or not having the treatment in question

atient is unable to use the information and weigh it in the
e as part of the process of arriving at the decision

Source: *Re MB. (an adult: medical treatment)* [1997]

12

Compulsory Caesarean sections

Box 12.1: Case scenario

Miss MB. required a Caesarean section in order to save her fetus. However, while she gave consent to the operation, she suffered from a needle phobia which caused her to panic and refuse the preliminary anaesthetic. The trust applied for a declaration that the Caesarean section could take place on the grounds that the needle phobia rendered her mentally incapacitated and therefore the operation should proceed in her best interests (*Re MB. (an adult: medical treatment)* [1997]).

Introduction

It is the inalienable right of mentally competent adults to make their own decisions on treatment. Even if they refuse life-saving treatment, their refusal must be respected. This principle was upheld by the Court of Appeal in the case of *Re T. (adult: refusal of medical treatment)* (1992). Where, however, a person is considered on reasonable grounds to lack the necessary mental capacity then action can be taken out of necessity in their best interests. In the case of Re T., the Court of Appeal ruled that health professionals should check, where life-saving treatment was being refused, that the patient had the necessary mental capacity to refuse (see *p. 132*). In this chapter we look at how these principles apply in the case of pregnant women and what rights, if any, the fetus has in the decision-making process.

The case of Re S.

Mrs S., aged 30, was expecting her third child (*Re S. (adult: refusal of medical treatment)* (1992)). She was admitted with ruptured membranes and in spontaneous labour. She refused on religious grounds (she was described as a 'born again Christian') a Caesarean section and was supported by her husband in her refusal. The fetus was in a transverse lie and the obstetrician formed the view that a Caesarean section was a life-saving necessity both for Mrs S. and the child. The fetus could not be born alive without the Caesarean section. The health authority made an ex parte application (ie. the woman was not represented) to the Family Court. The application was made at 1.30 pm and the case heard at 2.00 pm. The judge, Sir Stephen Brown, who was President of the Family Division of the High Court, decided at 2.18 pm that the declaration could be made, authorising the surgeons and staff of a hospital to carry out an emergency Caesarean section operation upon Mrs S. The main grounds for the declaration was that the operation was in the vital interests of the woman and of her unborn child. The outcome was that the woman survived but the baby was stillborn.

Criticism of Re S.

This decision came under a lot of criticism since it appeared to place the pregnant woman in a different category than any other mentally competent adult. If a Caesarean section could be forced upon a mentally competent woman in the interests of the fetus, then compulsory control over a pregnant woman's smoking, drinking, drug taking and general lifestyle — all in the interests of the fetus — could be justified. Pregnant women would have a totally different legal status than any other mentally competent adult. S. herself did not appeal against the judge's decision to the Court of Appeal.

Other compulsory Caesa

Re S. was followed by sev
Caesarean section operations v
the woman. In one case, the
schizophrenia, was detained in
of the Mental Health Act 1983
section operation (*Tameside an*
1996). The consultant psychia
would lead to a profound deteri
and once the pregnancy was ov
psychotic medication which h
pregnancy because of dangers to
operation could proceed under s
1983 as being treatment for ment

This decision could be criti
for mental disorder was given too
section is considered to be treatme
difficult to find any treatment whic
mental state, would not come witl
mental disorder.

In a second case, a pregnant w
treatment and had had three previou
Caesarean section (*Norfolk and No*
W. [1996]). A consultant psychiatris
she was not suffering from mental
unable to balance the information gi
made to the court for a forceps delive
a Caesarean section. The judge de
evidence she lacked the mental comp
treatment. A declaration was made on

After th
need for clarit
Re MB.

Case of Re

In the case
mentally in
could theref
of Appeal u
capacity wa
which appl

Table 12.

A person l
functioning
consent to
occur whe

a. The p
is ma
havir

b. The
bala

Table 12.2: Principles laid down in Re MB. and incorporated in guidance issued by the Department of Health

1. The court is unlikely to entertain an application for a declaration unless the capacity of the patient to consent to or refuse the medical treatment is in issue

2. For the time being, at least, the doctors ought to seek a ruling from the High Court on the issue of competence

3. Those in charge should identify a potential problem as early as possible so that both the hospital and the patient can obtain legal advice

4. It is highly desirable that, in any case where it is not an emergency, steps are taken to bring it before the court, before it becomes an emergency, to remove the extra pressure from the parties and the court and to enable proper instructions to be taken, particularly from the patient and where possible give the opportunity for the court to hear oral evidence if appropriate

5. The hearing should be inter parties

6. The mother should be represented in all cases, unless, exceptionally, she does not wish to be. If she is unconscious she should have a guardian *ad litem*

7. The official solicitor should be notified of all applications to the High Court

8. There should in general be some evidence, preferably but not necessarily from a psychiatrist, as to the competence of the patient, if competence is in issue

9. Where time permits, the person identified to give the evidence as to capacity to consent to or refuse treatment should be made aware of the observations made by the Court of Appeal in this judgement

10. In order to be in a position to assess a patient's best interests the judge should be provided, if time allows, with information about the circumstances of a relevant background material about the patient

Source: Department of Health (1997)

The Court of Appeal emphasised that every person is presumed to have the capacity to consent to or to refuse medical treatment unless and until that presumption is rebutted. A competent woman who has the capacity to decide may, for religious reasons, other reasons, rational or irrational reasons or no reason at all, choose not to have medical intervention, even though the consequence may be the death or serious handicap of the child she bears, or her own death. In that event, the courts do not have the jurisdiction to declare medical intervention lawful and the question of her own best interests, objectively considered, does not arise.

Case of *St George's Healthcare NHS Trust* v. *S.*

The case of *St George's Healthcare NHS Trust* v. *S.*, *R.* v. *Collins ex parte S* (1998) reaffirmed the principles set out by the Court of Appeal in the case of Re MB. The facts were that a woman who was about thirty-six weeks pregnant was diagnosed as suffering from severe pre-eclampsia, severe oedema and proteinuria. She was advised to have early induction of labour as a life-saving necessity. She refused on the grounds that she would prefer to let nature take its course. She was then examined by an approved social worker and two doctors and was detained in hospital under section 2 of the Mental Health Act 1983. From there she was transferred to St George's Hospital for obstetric treatment. She was advised by a solicitor that she had the right to refuse treatment. The hospital applied in an ex parte application to the High Court judge stating that it was a life and death situation and the patient had gone into labour. This latter information was incorrect, and the judge was not informed that the patient had instructed solicitors. The judge made the declaration that S.'s consent could be dispensed with. S. was then given a Caesarean section. She was transferred back to the psychiatric hospital where a doctor decided that she was not suffering from mental disorder and took her off section 2, following which she took her own discharge.

The case eventually came before the Court of Appeal which emphasised the pregnant woman's right of self-determination, that the Mental Health Act should not have been used when a person was refusing treatment for hypertension, and stated that an unborn child is not a separate person from its mother.

Lord Justice Judge held that a pregnant woman is entitled not to be forced to submit to an invasion of her body against her will, whether her own life or that of her unborn child depends on it. Her right is not reduced or diminished merely because her decision to exercise it may appear morally repugnant. The declaration in this case involved the removal of the baby from within the body of her mother under physical compulsion. Unless lawfully justified, this constituted an infringement of the mother's autonomy. Of themselves, the perceived needs of the fetus did not provide the necessary justification.

The principles set out by the Court of Appeal in Re MB. were quoted in the case of Re B. (2002) (where a tetraplegic woman asked for her ventilator to be switched off; *Chapter 6, p. 55*).

The rights of the fetus

The unborn child is not recognised in law as having a legal personality. It is not until birth that the interests of the child can be taken into account. It can be seen from the above cases of Re MB. and the St George's Healthcare Trust that the interests of the unborn child cannot be raised against the wishes of a mentally competent mother. The mentally competent mother is entitled to make her autonomous decision whatever the outcome for her unborn child. If the mother makes a decision which harms the unborn child, so that the child is born with a disability or injury, the child has no legal right to sue the mother for breach of her duty of care to the child. Under the Congenital Disabilities (Civil Liability) Act 1976, if an unborn child has been injured so that it is born disabled, it can only sue the mother if the injuries were caused while the pregnant woman was driving a car. (In this case, of course, the mother would have third party insurance cover from which the injured child could benefit.) Any action against the mother (apart from one arising from these circumstances) brought by the child who was harmed while in utero is prevented by this Act. A child could not sue a mother who through drinking, taking drugs or smoking, caused harm to him or her while a fetus.

Conclusion

The cases of Re MB. and the St George's Healthcare Trust have clarified the law. The pregnant woman has the full right of autonomy as any other mentally competent adult. Some may find the disregard of the interests of the fetus to be morally unacceptable. However, the principles established by the Court of Appeal ensure that a pregnant woman is not simply treated as the carrier of a baby, but that her right of self-determination is protected in the same way as the right of self-determination of any other competent adult.

References

Department of Health (1997) Circular EL (97)32. DoH, London

Re B. (consent to treatment: capacity) The Times Law Report 26 March 2002.

Re MB. (an adult: medical treatment) [1997] 2 FLR 426

Re S. (adult: refusal of medical treatment)(1992) 9 BMLR 69 [1993] Fam 123

Re T. (adult: refusal of medical treatment) (1992) 9 BLMR 46 [1993] Fam 95

Norfolk and Norwich Healthcare (NHS) Trust v. *W.* [1996] 2 FLR 613

St George's Healthcare NHS Trust v. *S.*; *R.* v. *Collins ex parte S.* (1998) 44 BMLR 160 CA; [1998]3 All ER 673

Tameside and Glossop Acute Services Trust v. *CH* [1996] 1 FLR 762 (1996) 31 BMLR 93

13

Organ donation after death

Box 13.1: Case scenario

Tony has been severely injured in a road accident. He is twenty-three years old. His parents are told that he has serious brain damage and is unlikely to survive. They are asked if they would agree to the donation of his organs. What is the law?

Introduction

The law relating to the donation of organs after death is covered by the Human Tissue Act 1961. Donation from a living donor is covered by the Human Organ Transplants Act 1989 and commercial transactions involving organs are a criminal offence; this will be considered in the next chapter. This chapter considers the use of organs from a dead donor and the right to give consent.

Human Tissue Act 1961

The Act covers two distinct situations involving organ donation from a dead person: the first where the person has indicated his/her wishes over organ donation; and the second where there is no indication of a wish to be a donor and relatives are asked their views.

Wishes expressed by the donor

> ### Box 13.2: Section 1(1) of the Human Tissue Act
>
> If any person, either in writing at any time or orally in the presence of two or more witnesses during his last illness, has expressed a request that his body or any specified part of his body be used after his death for therapeutic purposes or for purposes of medical education or research, the person lawfully in possession of his body after his death may unless he has reason to believe that the request was subsequently withdrawn, authorise the removal from the body of any part or, as the case may be, the specified part, for use in accordance with the request.

Section 1(1) of the Human Tissue Act 1961 is shown in *Box 13.2*. Section 1(1) covers the situation of the person carrying the donor card. It also covers the situation where a dying person makes it clear before two witnesses that he/she would wish to donate his/her body, or any parts thereof, for other people or medical or research purposes. In this case, the relatives have a very limited role. They would only need to be contacted to discover if the dying person had subsequently withdrawn his/her wish to be a donor.

The person lawfully in possession of the body

The person lawfully in possession of the body, where a person dies in hospital, is initially the hospital trust board, and then the executors of the dead person's estate or the personal representatives. Section 1(7) of the Act states that:

In the case of a body lying in a hospital, nursing home or other institution, any authority under this section may be given on behalf of the person having the control and management thereof by any officer or person designated for that purposes by the first-mentioned person.

In the case of a road accident, the death would have to be reported to the coroner, who then has jurisdiction over the body, until such time as the coroner releases it. Any request for organ donation would have to be reported to and agreed with the coroner (Home Office, 1977). Where the executor of the estate has been identified, it could be argued that the executor then becomes the person lawfully in possession of the body and it is to be noted that the section states:

... person lawfully in possession of the body may... authorise.

This would appear to give some right for the executor to prevent the donation going ahead. The person lawfully in possession of the body does not (from the point of view of the Human Tissue Act 1961) have to accede to the wishes of the deceased.

Role of the relatives where deceased has expressed his/her wishes

Clearly, the relatives must be informed of the dead person's request, be asked if they know if the deceased had withdrawn his/her wish to be a donor but they have no right to overrule the deceased person's request. In practice, relatives, despite the deceased carrying a valid donor card, may object to organ donation and it is unlikely, particularly in the light of the recent events at Alder Hey Children's Hospital, Liverpool (DoH, 2001), that health professionals would insist upon the organs being harvested.

Death of the patient

Organs can only be taken after death has been certified and this should be by different doctors than those who wish to remove the organs. Guidelines from the Department of Health (1998) cover the diagnosis of brain death and the interpretation of the Human Tissue Act 1961. Since there is a much higher success in transplants where the organs are fresh, the body may be kept ventilated until such time as the organs can be harvested. What is the legality of this? Where the patient is in intensive care and on a ventilator and carries a donor card, it could be argued that he/she has expressly agreed to being ventilated until the organs are removed, even though this may be several hours after brainstem death has been diagnosed. This would not appear to be illegal. Slightly different considerations would arise when the patient has not expressed a wish to be a donor but the relatives have consented. It could be argued that the relatives implicitly agree that the ventilation can continue until such time as the organs can be taken.

A different practice was adopted in a district general hospital, where patients were transferred to intensive care when dying of a cerebrovascular accident (Feest *et al*, 1990). As a result, the team estimated that the donor rate increased from 19.8% to 37.5%. The practice has, however, been declared unlawful by the Department of Health, ie. where ventilation is not undertaken for the patient's own benefit (DoH, 1998).

Where no wishes have been expressed by the donor

> ## Box 13.3: Section 1(2) of the Human Tissue Act 1961
>
> Without prejudice to the foregoing subsection, the person lawfully in possession of the body of a deceased person may authorise the removal of any part from the body for use of the said purposes if, having made such reasonable enquiry as may be practicable, he has no reason to believe: that the deceased had expressed an objection to his body being so dealt with after his death and had not withdrawn it; or that the surviving spouse or any surviving relative of the deceased objects to the body being so dealt with.

Section 1(2) of the Human Tissue Act 1961 covers the situation where the dying person has not made his/her wishes about organ donation known (*Box 13.3*).

Where the deceased has not expressly wished to be a donor, the relatives have much greater powers. Reasonable enquiries, only so far as they are practicable, have to be made as to whether the deceased expressed any objection to being a donor and as to whether any relative objects.

There are different views as to what constitutes reasonable enquiries. Is it sufficient just to contact those who come to the hospital or should more remote relatives be contacted? There is no definition of 'any surviving relative', so in practice a remote relative who has minimum or even no contact with the deceased could block the organ donation if they came to hear of the possibility.

Where after reasonable enquiries the relatives are unknown or unavailable, it would be possible for authorisation to be given for the removal of the organs without their consent (DoH, 2000). However, it would seem wise in these times of extreme public sensitivity to the removal of organs that this occurs only in exceptional situations where the removal would be clearly justified.

Case scenario

Turning back to the situation in the case scenario, it would appear that Tony does not come under section 1(1) of the Human Tissue Act 1961, since he has made no express wish known, either in writing or by word of mouth. His relatives must be consulted under section 1(2) to ascertain if he has ever expressed objections to being a donor or if they object. In addition, since he was injured in a road accident, his death would have to be reported to the coroner. The coroner would be informed of the relatives' views and if they did not object, could give his/her consent to the organ removal.

Proposals for change

It is clear that the supply of organs is not meeting the needs of those awaiting organ transplants and many patients are dying on the waiting lists. In October 2000, 6000 persons were awaiting an organ transplant and many would die before one became available. One suggestion is that there should be an opting-out system, rather than an opting-in system, ie. carrying a card if you do not want your body to be used for transplant purposes, and the absence of a card implies an agreement to the organs being transplanted. However, this suggestion has not met with wide acceptance. An alternative suggestion is that there should be a legal duty for the professionals to request an organ transplant from the relatives of the deceased or prospective deceased. This is described as the required request system. It has the advantage of removing some of the embarrassment that professionals feel when they have to broach the matter with relatives. It is thought that such a statutory request would lead to more organs being forthcoming without the necessity for a change in the Human Tissue Act itself. The relatives would still have the freedom to refuse but they would also have the opportunity to agree.

A private member's bill was put before Parliament in April 2000 recommending that there should be an opting-out system, ie. there is a presumption that the deceased would consent to being a donor. This presumption could, however, be rebutted by evidence that the deceased would not wish to donate his/her organs. The bill was given its first reading, but did not proceed and it was never printed. An initiative supported by actors and actresses in the television soap drama *Coronation Street* was designed to increase the number of organ donors. Information for potential donors is given on a Department of Health website (www.nhs.uk/organdonor). It was followed by a scheme whereby credit card companies will ask customers applying for a card to sign up on the organ donor register (DoH, 2000).

The availability of organs declined after the publication of the report into the removal, retention and storage of organs at Alder Hey Children's Hospital (DoH, 2001). For example, the Royal Brompton Hospital, London, and the Queen Elizabeth Hospital, Birmingham, reported that in the twelve days, ending on 5 February 2001, they had not carried out a single transplant when normally they would carry out about three a week.

Changes in the law are necessary, but these can only be made once public confidence in the medical profession is restored. In the next chapter we consider donation by living donors. A consultation paper (Human Bodies and Human Choices) has been issued to consider possible changes in the law (see *page 125*).

References

Department of Health (1998) *Code of Practice for the Diagnosis of Brain Death*. DoH, London. Online at: http://www.nhs.uk/organdonor

Department of Health (2000) *Credit Cards to Promote Organ Donation*. DoH, London

Department of Health (2001) *The Royal Liverpool's Children's Inquiry Report*. DoH, London

Feest TG, Riad HN, Collins CH *et al* (1990) Protocol for increasing organ donation after cerebrovascular deaths in a district general hospital. *Lancet* **335**: 1133–5

Home Office (1977) Home Office Circular 1977/65. Home Office, London

14

Organ donation from live donors

Box 14.1: Case scenario

Alice is now twelve years old and has been receiving dialysis for over three years. Her long-term chance of survival depends upon a kidney transplant and she has been on a waiting list for several years. Her condition is deteriorating and Bob, a close friend of her family, has offered to donate her a kidney. What is the law?

Introduction

Under section 1(1) of the Human Organ Transplants Act 1989, the commercial dealings with human organs is a criminal offence, as shown in *Table 14.1*.

Section 1(2) of the 1989 Act prohibits advertising for the supply of organs. Section 1(3) excludes from these criminal offences the cost of removing, transporting or preserving organs to be supplied and also any expenses or loss of earnings incurred by a person so far as reasonable and directly attributable to his/her supplying an organ from his/her body.

However, the Human Organ Transplants Act 1989 does not prevent the *bona fide* gift of organs and the reimbursement of costs incurred in transporting and the reasonable expenses of the donor. It is also significant that the 1989 Act covers organs from the living and the dead, so commercial dealing in organs from deceased persons is also made a criminal offence.

Table 14.1: Human Organ Transplants Act 1989 (section 1(1))

A person is guilty of an offence if in Great Britain he/she:

a. Makes or receives payment for the supply of, or for an offer to supply, an organ which has been or is to be removed from a dead or living person and is intended to be transplanted into another person whether in Great Britain or elsewhere

b. Seeks to find a person willing to supply for payment such an organ as is mentioned in paragraph (a) above or offers to supply such an organ for payment

c. Initiates or negotiates any arrangement involving the making of any payment for the supply of, or for an offer to supply, such an organ

d. Takes part in the management or control of a body of persons corporate or unincorporated whose activities consist of or include the initiation or negotiations of such arrangements

'Organ'

The 1989 Act only covers the donation of organs. It does not make the sale of regeneratable parts or tissue a criminal offence. 'Organ' is defined in section 7(2) of the Act as:

> *Any part of a human body consisting of a structured arrangement of tissues which, if wholly removed, cannot be replicated by the body.*

Thus, the contract between Alder Hey Hospital, Liverpool, and a pharmaceutical company, that the former would supply thymus glands from the bodies of dead children and the company would, in return, provide some payment, would not be prevented by the 1989 Act. It is a different question as to whether the parents gave or would have given consent for such a transaction, and this is considered in the next chapter.

Transfer of organs from a living person

The 1989 Act, section 2, makes it a criminal offence for a person to remove an organ from a living person or transplant it into another person unless the donor and donee are genetically related (*Table 14.2*).

Table 14.2: Human Organ Transplants Act 1989 (section 2(1))
Subject to subsection (3), a person is guilty of an offence in Great Britain if he/she:
a. Removes from a living person an organ intended to be transplanted into another person, or
b. Transplants an organ removed from a living person into another person. Unless the person into whom the organ is to be or, as the case may be, is transplanted is genetically related to the person from whom the organ is removed

'Genetically related'

The words 'genetically related' are defined in section 2(2) of the Act. A person is genetically related to:

a. His natural parents and children.
b. His brothers and sisters of the whole or half blood.
c. The brothers and sisters of the whole or half blood of either of his natural parents.
d. The natural children of his brothers and sisters of the whole or half blood or of the brothers and sisters of the whole or half blood of either of his natural parents.

This genetic relationship must be confirmed by appropriate tests set up under regulations from the Secretary of State (Human Organ Transplants, 1989a). Doctors commit a criminal offence if the relationship has not been confirmed in the appropriate manner.

Transplants from people who are not genetically related

Under section 2(3) of the 1989 Act, the Secretary of State has the power to make regulations to permit transplants from persons who are not genetically related, provided that no payment has been or is to be made. Under regulations made under this section, the Unrelated Live Transplant Regulatory Authority (ULTRA) has been established (Human Organ Transplants, 1989b). Before ULTRA can agree to a transplant from a genetically unrelated person, ULTRA must be satisfied that:

a. No payment has been, or is to be, made in contravention of section 1 of the Act.
b. That the registered medical practitioner who has caused the matter to be referred to the Authority has clinical responsibility for the donor.
c. Except in a case where the primary purpose of the removal of an organ from a donor is the medical treatment of that donor, that the conditions specified in paragraph 2 of this regulation are satisfied.

The conditions referred to in paragraph c of the regulations are shown in *Table 14.3*.

An example of a situation where the organ may be removed for the medical treatment of the donor is shown in *Box 14.2*.

Table 14.3: Conditions where the donor does not require the removal of the organ for medical treatment

a. That a registered medical practitioner has given the donor an explanation of the nature of the medical procedure for, and the risk involved in, the removal of the organ in question

b. That the donor understands the nature of the medical procedure and the risks, as explained by the registered medical practitioner, and consents to the removal of the organ in question

c. That the donor's consent to the removal of the organ in question was not obtained by coercion or the offer of an inducement

d. That the donor understands that he is entitled to withdraw his consent if he wishes, but has not done so

e. That the donor and the recipient have both been interviewed by a person who appears to the Authority to have been suitably qualified to conduct such interviews and who has reported to the Authority on the conditions contained in subparagraphs a to d above and has included in his report an account of any difficulties of communication with the donor or the recipient and an explanation of how those difficulties were overcome

In the situation in *Box 14.2*, the high probability is that none of these three persons would be genetically related. Previous permission would be required from ULTRA to the possibility of Glen's heart being transferred to a patient requiring a heart transplant. This permission would be sought as soon as Glen was placed on the waiting list. The full consent conditions set out in *Table 14.3* would not be satisfied. Hopefully, however, in practice, when Glen agreed to a transplant his voluntary consent, without coercion or inducement, would be obtained and full information given as discussed in *Chapters 4* and *5* of this book.

> **Box 14.2: Organ donation for medical purposes**
>
> Glen suffered from cystic fibrosis and had been on the waiting list for a lung transplant for over two years. At the hospital, surgeons transplanted either lungs or both heart and lungs. A decision was not made definitely on the type of transplant until organs became available. When the patient was opened up, the surgeons would then decide whether to transplant both heart and lungs or merely the lungs. In the event of both heart and lungs being transplanted, it may be that the heart, provided that it was not diseased, could be available for transplant for another person. Glen was asked if he would agree to his heart being available for transplant in the event of his receiving both heart and lungs.

Alice's gift

Turning now to the situation shown in the case scenario shown in *Box 14.1*, this transplant would be governed by the regulations relating to transplants from genetically unrelated persons.

In this case, Bob would have to be interviewed and all the conditions set out in *Table 14.3* satisfied. There must be no payment given or promised and no other inducement (eg. a condition that Alice's widowed mother would marry Bob, the donor, if he gave Alice his kidney would clearly invalidate the gift and make it illegal under the 1989 Act).

Another consequence of the conditions set out in *Table 14.3* is that a person who is mentally incapable of giving consent cannot provide an organ for a person to whom he/she is not genetically related. The 1989 Act does not permit any such decision to be made on behalf of a mentally incapacitated adult.

In contrast, where transplants between genetically related persons are in question, these are not regulated by ULTRA and the conditions of consent set out in *Table 14.3* do not apply, so it would be possible for the court to make a declaration that such a transplant from a mentally incapacitated adult was in the best interests of the latter.

In *Chapter 11* the case of Re Y. (1996) was discussed where the court was asked to make a declaration that blood tests and bone marrow harvesting were in the best interests of the mentally incapacitated sister. Since these did not come under the definition of organ in section 7(2), this was outside the provisions of the 1989 Act.

Conclusion

There are many anomalies in this field. The law has provided some protection from exploitation. There would appear to be nothing to prevent a UK citizen going abroad and buying an organ for transplant and having the operation performed overseas, as long as it did not break the laws of that country. It could be questioned why the law provides such clear protection for those who are not genetically related, and very little for those who are genetically related. Could not family pressures lead to an offer to donate an organ? Why should the consent provisions not apply to all donors, whether they are genetically related, and whether or not the organs are removed because of medical treatment? Is there not also justification for similar laws covering the donation of regenerative parts?

Perhaps the law will eventually have to be modified when the scientific development of growing organs and spare body parts has been perfected. In the next chapter we look at the question of organ removal, retention and storage.

References

Human Organ Transplants (1989a) (Establishment of Relationship) Regulations SI 1989 No 2107

Human Organ Transplants (1989b) (Unrelated Persons) Regulations SI 1989 No 2480

Re Y. (1996) (adult patient) (transplant: bone marrow) 35 BMLR 111; 4 Med LR 204

15

Organ removal, retention, storage

Box 15.1: Case scenario

Sarah was born with a congenital heart condition. Unfortunately, the subsequent operation proved unsuccessful and Sarah died. Sarah's parents were asked if they would agree to a postmortem being performed to assist in research so that in future such conditions could be successfully operated upon. The parents agreed and subsequently they were notified that the body was available for disposal. They decided upon a cremation. Several years later, following an inquiry into the pathology services of the hospital, they were notified by the Chief Executive's department that Sarah's heart, lungs, liver and other organs had been retained. The parents were shocked. What is the law?

Introduction

Unfortunately, the situation in the above 'case scenario' box confronted many patients across the country, as evidenced in the reports of the Bristol Royal Infirmary (DoH, 2000; 2001a) inquiry and the Royal Liverpool's Children's (Alder Hey) inquiry (DoH, 2001b) on the retention of organs and body parts. During the Bristol Royal Infirmary inquiry into allegations of professional misconduct in carrying out paediatric heart surgery, it was learnt that human organs from children who had died had been retained. The publication of the Alder Hey report coincided with publication of a report of a census of organs and tissues retained by pathology services in England (DoH, 2001c).

Census of organs and tissues retained by pathology services

The conclusion from the census of retained organs and tissue is that a total of approximately 54,300 organs, body parts, stillbirths or fetuses were held by pathology services at the end of 1999. They had been retained from postmortems over the period 1970–1999. (This does not include the numbers held following a postmortem ordered by a coroner.) The census concluded that retention of organs, tissue and body parts after postmortem was commonplace throughout the country and in the majority of cases was based on a consent form signed under the Human Tissue Act 1961. The census report listed the different pathology departments across England and the numbers of parts which they held.

The law

The Anatomy Act 1984 (and the 1988 Regulations under the Act) enable people to bequeath their bodies for anatomical examination by dissection for teaching, studying or research purposes. There are specific provisions for the disposal of the body and the Act is administered by Her Majesty's Inspector of Anatomy. In contrast to the Anatomy Act, the Human Tissue Act 1961 (*Chapter 13*), does not have any regulatory framework of any penalties for non-compliance. Under the Human Tissue Act, where the deceased has not expressed any views, the person in lawful possession of the body is required to make reasonable enquiries to establish whether the deceased had any objection to the use of his/her parts of his/her body or whether any surviving relatives objected to such a use. The purposes for such removal include; therapeutic purposes, or the purposes of medical education or research.

In the case of babies and young children, there would, of course, be no views expressed. The relatives, usually the parents, would have to give consent to the postmortem being carried out (except where the coroner required the postmortem to take place, see below) and also to the removal and retention of organs. From the census carried out by the Chief Medical Officer it was learnt that 97% of trusts during 1999 used forms to obtain a signed agreement from relatives for post-mortems and 86% used the same form for retention of organs or tissues after hospital postmortem. Six per cent used a separate form to record agreement to retention of organs or tissues. However, in the 1970s, 1980s and early 1990s, parents were not given full information in relation to which organs were to be removed and retained and explicit consent was not obtained.

Advice on organ retention

In 1977, the Department of Health and Social Security (DHSS) provided a postmortem declaration form to ensure that inquiries of relatives were made not only as to any relevant objection to the postmortem examination itself, but also to the removal and retention of tissue (DHSS, 1977). Subsequently, in 1999, the Royal College of Pathologists issued a consensus statement on the use of human tissue in research, education and quality control (Royal College of Pathologists and Institute of Bio-Medical Science, 1999) and also guidelines for the retention of tissues and organs at postmortem examination (Royal College of Pathologists, 2000). In October 2000, the British Medical Association (BMA) issued advice to its members that relatives should give informed consent to the retention of organs. It should also be made clear that relatives can refuse consent to a postmortem examination, unless it has been ordered by a coroner (BMA, 2000).

Coroner's postmortem

Where the coroner requires a postmortem to complete an inquiry into the cause of death, the parents and relatives do not have the right to refuse. Special provisions in the Human Tissue Act 1961 and under the Coroners' Rules (1984) apply. Section 1(5) of the Human Tissue Act 1961 states that:

> *Where a person has reason to believe that an inquest may be required to be held on any body or that a postmortem examination of any body may be required by the coroner, he shall not, except with the consent of the coroner: give an authority under this section in respect of the body, or act on such an authority given by any other person.*

The Coroners' Rules require material removed from the body to be preserved for such period as the coroner thinks fit.

In the census of the Chief Medical Officer, it was found that 16,000 retained organs and body parts resulted from coroners' postmortems. Tissue samples were retained from about 800,000 coroners' postmortems. The retention of organs after a coroner's postmortem is not provided for under the coroners' legislation and any retention following the ending of the coroner's inquiry should come under the provisions of the Human Tissue Act 1961. In the census it was found that the basis for retention included written or verbal consent from relatives, tradition, and a verbal or blanket authority from the coroner.

At the same time that the Alder Hey Inquiry report was published the Department of Health published a report on an analysis of NHS trust policies and protocols on consent to organ and tissue retention at postmortem examination and disposal of human materials as part of the census by the Chief Medical Officer (DoH, 2001d). The aim was to assist the Chief Medical Officer in providing further guidance to the NHS.

Advice from the Chief Medical Officer on the removal,

retention and use of human organs and tissue from postmortem examination proposed a new approach aimed at commanding public confidence and paying proper respect to the feelings and rights of bereaved relatives for information and informed consent (DoH, 2001e).

The report summarises the nature and scope of current and past practice in relation to the retention of organs and tissues; draws together the main problems and concerns which have arisen from the operation of the system to date; and recommends comprehensive changes to current practice to ensure a proper respect for the person who has died and the surviving relatives, compassionate treatment of bereaved families and clear information and full explanations to be given by clinicians on the purposes of organ tissue removal and retention (DoH, 2001e).

The aim is to secure effective participation by families in taking key decisions so that with the support of the public, the benefits of greater understanding of disease through research, audit and teaching, using retained tissue and organs after death, will help future generations of patients.

Retained Organs Commission

The Government has set up a Retained Organs Commission under the Chairmanship of Professor Margaret Brazier. It is a special health authority with specific functions (*Table 15.1*). In addition, it advises ministers and provides guidance to the NHS and universities and monitor trusts to ensure that they deal properly with organ returns. It also provides a national help line via NHS Direct for parents and relatives. At the end of April 2001, the Chair of the Retained Organs Commission announced that trusts were to begin to release information to people who have made inquiries about whether organs from relatives have been retained following postmortems (DoH, 2001f).

In September 2002, the first annual report of the Retained

Organs Commission was published and it was announced that the Commission's existence would be extended to 31 March 2004 in order that it could complete its work.

Table 15.1: Functions of the Retained Organs Commission
• Oversee the return of tissues and organs from collections around the country
• Ensure that collections are accurately catalogued
• Provide information on collections throughout the country
• Ensure that suitable counselling is available
• Act as an advocate for parents if problems arise
• Advise on good practice in this area
• Handle inquiries from families and the public

Case scenario

It is clear from the evidence which has emerged from the inquiries and census that many hospitals were not giving full information to relatives when the latter gave consent for a postmortem to be undertaken. Like Sarah's parents in *Box 15.1*, relatives signed consent for a postmortem but were not given the information about which organs were removed and retained. From a legal point of view, although the Human Tissue Act 1961 does not explicitly permit the removal and retention of tissues, it has been interpreted as implying that 'authorisation of a postmortem examination can be taken to include authorisation for the removal and retention of some tissue' (Kennedy and Grubb, 2000). If this is a correct interpretation of the law it is unlikely that Sarah's parents would have any legal action against the hospital for the retention of the organs.

However, it was announced on 10 November 2000 that families of dead children whose organs were removed or kept without their permission had begun legal action against the hospital where they died (*The Times*, 2000). Four families are suing the Diana, Princess of Wales Children's Hospital in Birmingham for the unlawful removal, retention and disposal of human tissue and for misleading them as to the extent of the practice. At the time of writing, the results of this action are unknown. Sarah's parents may have a claim under the Human Rights Act 1998 that they have been subjected to inhuman and degrading treatment under Article 3 of the European Convention on Human Rights.

Future changes to the law

The Government's intention is to bring in legal changes to amend the Human Tissue Act, to make it an explicit requirement that the informed consent of the parents or relatives must be obtained for the postmortem to be carried out and for the removal, and retention of organs or tissues. The possibility of making it a criminal offence to fail to comply with the legal requirements is also being considered and this question of introducing a criminal offence is one of the questions specifically raised in a consultation paper on the law relating to human organs and tissues issued in July 2002 by the Department of Health and the Wales National Assembly (DoH, 2002). The Consultation Report envisages that there will be legislation to ensure that in general organs and tissue should be removed, retained or used only for purposes for which those concerned have had the opportunity to give their valid consent. (An exception would be where the coroner has ordered a postmortem examination.) The Consultation ended in October 2002 and draft legislation (or a White Paper) is at the time of writing anticipated.

Conclusions

Paternalistic medicine where information is kept from patients and parents supposedly for their own good and where research interests take precedence over the interests and concerns of relatives is no longer acceptable. The emphasis now must be on communication, real informed consent, and bereavement support, with obligations clearly set out in the law. One of the great tragedies in this scandal is the loss of public confidence in doctors and health professionals. Donor cards are being torn up, many more people on waiting lists for transplants will die before organs become available, and essential medical research will be inhibited. There is a major challenge for all health professionals, health trusts and the Department of Health to rebuild public confidence so that *bona fide* research, and organ donation for transplants can take place. Speedy changes to the law, following the consultation process, will support this rebuilding of confidence.

References

British Medical Association (2000) *Consent to Organ Retention*. BMA, London

Coroners' Rules (1984) SI 1984, No 552, Rule 9. The Stationery Office, London

Department of Health and Social Security (1977) *Postmortem Declaration Forms*. HC(77)28. DHSS, London

Department of Health (2000) The Inquiry into the Management of Care of Children Receiving Complex Heart Surgery at the Bristol Royal Infirmary. Interim Report: Removal and Retention of Human Material. DoH, London

Department of Health (2001a) The Report of the Public Inquiry into Children's Heart Surgery at the Bristol Royal Infirmary 1984–1995: Learning from Bristol. The Stationery Office, London

Department of Health (2001b) The Royal Liverpool's Children's Inquiry: Summary and Recommendations. Chaired by Michael Redfern QC. 30 January. The Stationery Office, London

Department of Health (2001c) *Chief Medical Officer: A Report of a Census of Organs and Tissues Retained by Pathology Services in England*. DoH, London

Department of Health (2001d) *Consent to Organ and Tissue Retention at Postmortem Examination and Disposal of Human Materials*. DoH, London

Department of Health (2001e) *The Removal, Retention and use of Human Organs and Tissue from Postmortem Examination. Advice from the Chief Medical Officer*. DoH, London: January

Department of Health (2001f) *NHS trusts ready to respond on retained organs*. (Press release.) DoH, London: 27 April

Department of Health (2002) *Human Bodies, Human Choices: The law on human organs and tissue in England and Wales. A consultation report*. Department of Health and Wales National Assembly

Kennedy I, Grubb A (2000) *Medical Law*. 3rd edn. Butterworths, London

Royal College of Pathologists (2000) *Guidelines for the Retention of Tissues and Organs at Post-mortem Examination*. RCP, London

Royal College of Pathologists and Institute of Bio-Medical Science (1999) *Consensus Statement of Recommended Policies for Uses of Human Tissue in Research, Education and Quality Control. (With notes reflecting UK law and practices.)* Working Party of the RCP and the Institute of Bio-Medical Science, London

The Times (2000) Parents sue hospital over organs. *The Times*, 10 November: 15

16

Living wills and the common law

Box 16.1: Case scenario

Since watching a programme on dementia on the television, Sam had always been terrified of losing his mental faculties. He therefore told his daughter that if he ever suffered from a disease which led to mental incapacity he would not wish to have any treatment. Some years later early signs of motor neurone's disease appeared and his condition worsened rapidly. He became incapable of swallowing and his mind deteriorated, so he was no longer able to express his views. His daughter told the healthcare staff at the hospital about his previous wishes and said that he would not wish to be fed artificially. Would staff be justified in giving him artificial feeding, contrary to the daughter's views?

Introduction

It is a basic principle of the law on consent that a mentally competent person can refuse treatment for a good reason, a bad reason or for no reason at all (*Re MB. (adult medical treatment)* [1997]). It is also an accepted principle that where a person has, when mentally competent, declared his/her wishes for a time when he/she may lack the mental capacity, then those previously declared views are binding upon health professionals caring for him/her during that time of incapacity. These earlier expressed views are variously known as a 'living will', an 'advanced directive' or an 'advance refusal of treatment'. At present there is no statute relating to such advance statements, but the law derives from decided cases (ie. judge-made law also known as the common law).

The law on advance statements

In 1993, the House of Lords discussed the situation relating to the discontinuation of artificial feeding for Tony Bland, the victim of the Hillsborough stadium disaster who was in a persistent vegetative state (*Airedale NHS Trust* v. *Bland* [1993]). It decided that the artificial feeding could be discontinued in his best interests. It also stated that had he made an advanced directive setting out his wishes if he were to become mentally incapacitated, then that directive would have been binding upon the health professionals caring for him.

A typical example of an advanced directive is the card carried by Jehovah's Witnesses. This makes it clear to what the person is refusing and it is signed by both the person refusing the treatment in anticipation, and by another person as a witness.

In the Canadian case of *Malette* v. *Shulman* (1990), an unconscious woman who was given a life-saving blood transfusion, in spite of the fact that she was carrying a card, won Canadian $20000 against the doctor. The reason was that the doctor was guilty of trespass to the person (ie. battery) in treating her against her express instructions even though she was then mentally incompetent.

The House of Lords in the Tony Bland case gave approval to the decision in this Canadian case, saying that if the same facts were to occur in this country, such treatment contrary to the advanced directive of the patient would be actionable in law. In the Tony Bland case, Lord Goff stated that:

> *[Respect must be given to the patient's wishes] where the patient's refusal to give his consent has been expressed at an*

earlier date, before he became unconscious or otherwise incapable of communicating it; though in such circumstances special care may be necessary to ensure that the prior refusal of consent is still properly to be regarded as applicable in the circumstances which have subsequently occurred.

Health professionals, therefore, have a duty in law to respect the living will or advance refusal of treatment if it applies to the present situation of a mentally incapacitated adult and was made at a time when the person did have the necessary mental capacity.

How should an advance directive be drawn up?

At common law there are no specific requirements as to the drawing up of a living will. The important points are that there should be clear evidence as to:

- the fact that the person is mentally capable at the time he/she expresses his/her advance refusal
- what his/her refusal consists of
- that this is intended to be binding at a later time when he/she lacks the capacity
- that there is a witness to this directive.

Unlike an ordinary will, which to be valid must satisfy very strict requirements under the Wills Act 1837 as amended, there is at present no statutory provisions governing the validity of living wills, so judges have the discretion at common law to decide what they would consider to be valid or not.

Guidance contained in the British Medical Association's (BMA's) code of practice on advance statements (BMA, 1995) has been specifically commended by the Law Commission (Law Commission, 1995) and by the Government (Lord Chancellor's Office, 1999). This code of practice suggests the minimum information which should be contained in a living will and the value of the name of a person who could speak on behalf of the person who made the living will. It suggests that, as a minimum, the following information is included:

- full name
- address
- name and address of GP
- whether advice was sought from health professionals
- signature
- date drafted and reviewed
- witness signature
- a clear statement of the person's wishes, either general or specific
- the name, address and telephone number of the nominated person, if there is one.

Has Sam created an advance directive?

The difficulty with Sam's expression of his wishes to his daughter is that they lack the certainty that a living will requires to be valid:

- it is not clear that they would refer to the situation which arose when he suffered from motor neurone's disease
- there is no evidence that these wishes were repeated at the time of the early stages of this illness
- there is no evidence that he wished to put these words in writing
- how do the health professionals know that Sam's daughter is telling the truth?

In the case of Re T. (which is considered in *Box 16.2*), Lord Donaldson warned against reliance upon the wishes of relatives when a patient lacks the requisite mental capacity:

*There seems to be a view in the medical profession that in...
emergency circumstances the next of kin should be asked to
consent on behalf of the patient and that, if possible,
treatment should be postponed until that consent has been
obtained. This is a misconception because the next of kin has
no legal right either to consent or to refuse consent.*

**Box 16.2: Case of *Re T. (adult: refusal of medical treatment)*
[1992]**

T., thirty-four weeks pregnant, was injured in a road accident. She
had been brought up by her mother who was a Jehovah's Witness,
although she was not herself a member of that religion. After being
alone with her mother, she told the staff nurse that she would not
want to have a blood transfusion. At that time, it was unlikely that
it would become necessary. Shortly afterwards she went into
labour and it was agreed that she would have a Caesarean section.
Again, after being alone with her mother, she told the medical staff
that she did not want to have a blood transfusion. She signed a
form of refusal of consent to a blood transfusion. It was not
explained to her that it might be necessary to give her a blood
transfusion to save her life. Following the Caesarean section, the
doctors, in compliance with her wishes, did not give her blood and
she was placed on a ventilator and paralysing drugs were
administered. Her father (who was not a Jehovah's Witness) and
her boyfriend applied to the court for a declaration that it was
lawful to give her a blood transfusion. The High Court judge held at
the first hearing that it was lawful for a blood transfusion to be
given and at the second hearing that T. had neither consented to,
nor refused, a blood transfusion in the emergency which had arisen
and it was therefore lawful for the doctors to treat her in whatever
way they considered, in the exercise of their professional
judgement, to be in her best interests.

(Re T. (adult: refusal of medical treatment) [1992])

Absence of a valid advance directive

If it is considered that there are significant doubts as to whether or not the patient has made a clear advance refusal of treatment, then the patient would have to be treated as a mentally incapacitated adult. In such a case, care must be provided in the best interests of the patient according to the common law power to act out of necessity recognised by the House of Lords in the Re F. case (*Re F. (a mental patient: sterilisation)* [1990]).

Where a document has been drawn up, but there are reasonable doubts as to its validity as an advanced refusal, then a declaration from the court could be sought and treatment given in the meantime, to keep the patient alive until the court's decision was made known.

There are considerable advantages in staff discussing with patients who are at an early stage of a deteriorating illness, but while they still enjoy their mental capacity, their views on active intervention. Clearly, this topic would have to be broached sensitively and the correct time chosen for such communication. It would certainly be preferable to relying entirely upon the relatives telling staff what the patient would not have wished, when this can no longer be confirmed with the patient.

The problem over what constituted a valid refusal arose in the case of Re T. (*Box 16.2*). T. appealed to the Court of Appeal. The Court of Appeal held that T.'s refusal was the result of her mother's undue influence upon her and was invalid. In addition, when she signed the form of refusal (the design of which was criticised by Lord Donaldson) she did so in ignorance of the particular circumstances which later arose (ie. that blood may be needed in a life-saving situation for herself).

Advice from the Lord Chancellor's Office

In *Chapter 7* we discussed the fact that the Lord Chancellor has initiated a consultation paper of several leaflets which are to be issued to different groups who are involved in decision making by people who have difficulty deciding for themselves (Lord Chancellor's Department Consultation Paper, 2002). Leaflet 6 is a guide for people wishing to plan for future incapacity. It covers the following topics:

- who is this leaflet aimed at?
- the right to make your own decisions?
- what is capacity?
- what can I do to plan for future incapacity?
- what decisions can't be delegated?
- how should decisions be made on my behalf?
- safeguards against abuse?
- further information.

Conclusion

There is a difference between a relative reporting what he/she considers the patient would or not wish to happen and an advance refusal or living will by a patient. An advanced refusal must be clearly intended to be operative in the circumstances which arise when the patient becomes mentally incapacitated. There are considerable uncertainties about the common law and its application to advanced refusals. It is hoped that the consultation on leaflets will not lead to further delays in the publishing of statutory proposals for decision making on behalf of mentally incapacitated adults. The next chapter will consider the Law Commission's proposals for statutory provisions and the Government's response.

References

Airedale NHS Trust v. *Bland* [1993] 1 All ER 821

British Medical Association (1995) *Advance Statements About Medical Treatment.* BMA, London

Law Commission (1995) *Mental Incapacity.* Report No 231. The Stationery Office, London

Lord Chancellor's Department (2002) *Making Decisions: Helping People who have Difficulty Deciding for Themselves.* Consultation Paper. Online at: http://www.lcd.gov.uk/consult/family/decision.htm

Lord Chancellor's Office (1999) *Making Decisions: The Government's Proposals for Making Decisions on Behalf of Mentally Incapacitated Adults.* The Stationery Office, London

Malette v. *Shulman* (1990) 67 DLR (4th) 321

Re F. (a mental patient: sterilisation) [1990] 2 AC 1

Re MB. (adult medical treatment) [1997] 2 FLR 426

Re T. (adult: refusal of medical treatment) [1992] 4 All ER 649 (1992) 9 BMLR 46 CA

17

Statutory provisions and living wills

Box 17.1: Case scenario

Mary had cared for her invalid mentally infirm mother for many years and was determined that if she ever lost her own mental capacity she would not wish to be kept alive. She drew up a document, witnessed by her sister, that stated in the event of her suffering from any form of mental incapacity she would not wish to be fed or have any medical or nursing intervention. Some years later she began to suffer from the early signs of Alzheimer's disease. Her sister had died, but staff were aware that Mary still carried this living will on her person. She is now refusing all food. What is the law?

Introduction

The last chapter set out the basic principles on the common law relating to living wills. It was noted that a person could refuse, in advance, treatments and procedures which are contemplated at a time when that person lacks the mental capacity to make his/her own decisions. In 1995, the Law Commission (an independent body which reviews our laws) published its final proposals on establishing a framework for decision making on behalf of mentally incompetent adults (Law Commission, 1995). The recommendations contained draft legislation which could have been put before Parliament. The Mental Incapacity Bill contained a clause covering the legal changes relating to advance refusal of treatment.

The Law Commission's proposals for draft legislation included, in clause nine, statutory provision covering: the definition of an advance refusal of treatment; the contents of an advance refusal; exclusions from living wills; referral to court if doubt about validity; and legal position of health professional. A summary of clause nine is shown in *Table 17.1*.

The Mental Incapacity Bill proposed by the Law Commission was not placed before Parliament, but in 1997 the Lord Chancellor issued a consultation document (Lord Chancellor, 1997). The consultation period ended on 31 March 1998 and in October 1999 the Government published its proposals (Lord Chancellor, 1999).

In relation to advance statements, it considered that in the light of the wide range of views on this complex and sensitive subject and given the flexibility inherent in developing case law, the Government believes that it would not be appropriate to legislate at the present time and thus fix the statutory position once and for all. In rejecting the need for a statute covering living wills, the Government stated for the clarity of lawyers, doctors and patients what it perceives to be the present position in law:

> *The current law and medical practice is as follows. It is a principle of law and medical practice that all adults have the right to consent to or refuse medical treatment. Advance statements are a means for patients to exercise that right by anticipating a time when they may lose the capacity to make or communicate a decision.*

(Lord Chancellor, 1999, paragraph 16)

Paragraphs 17–20 expand on this statement by making it clear that if the advance statement requests specific treatments this does not legally bind a health professional to act contrary to his/her professional judgement. Advance statements do not permit euthanasia 'which is and will remain illegal'.

Table 17.1: Clause nine of the 1995 Law Commission report

9(1)   In this Act an 'advance refusal of treatment' means refusal by a person who has attained the age of eighteen and has the necessary capacity of any medical, surgical or dental treatment or other procedure, being a refusal intended to have effect at any subsequent time when he may be without capacity to give or refuse his consent

9(2)   Section 4 (which is the general authority to act on behalf of those who lack mental capacity) does not authorise any such treatment or procedure as is mentioned in subsection (1) above if an advance refusal of treatment by the person concerned applies to that treatment or procedure in the circumstances of the case (ie. where there is a living will which applies, then the general power to act on behalf of the mentally incapacitated adult does not apply)

9(3)   In the absence of any indication to the contrary, it shall be presumed that an advance refusal of treatment does not apply in circumstances where those having the care of the person who made it consider that the refusal endangers that person's life; or if that person is a woman who is pregnant, the life of the foetus

9(4)   No person shall incur any liability for the consequences of withholding any treatment or procedure if he has reasonable grounds for believing that an advance refusal of treatment by the person concerned applies to that treatment or procedure; or for carrying out any treatment or procedure to which an advance refusal of treatment by the person concerned applies unless he knows, or has reasonable grounds for believing, that an advance refusal of treatment by the person concerned applies to the treatment or procedure

9(5)   Without prejudice to any other method of expressing an advance refusal of treatment, such a refusal may take the form of an instrument in writing; and in the absence of any indication to the contrary, it shall be presumed that an advance refusal of treatment was validly made if it takes the form of an instrument in writing which is signed by the person by whom it is made and by at least one other person as a witness to his signature

9(6)   An advance refusal of treatment may at any time be withdrawn or altered by the person who made it, if he then has the capacity to do so

9(7)   Notwithstanding the foregoing provisions, an advance refusal of treatment shall not preclude: the provision for the person who made it of basic care; or the taking of any action necessary to prevent his death or serious deterioration in his condition pending a decision of the court on the validity or applicability of an advance refusal of treatment or on the question whether it has been withdrawn or altered

9(8)   In subsection 7a above, 'basic care' means care to maintain bodily cleanliness and to alleviate severe pain and the provision of direct oral nutrition and hydration

While the Government applauded the flexibility of the common law in dealing with advance statements, there are several disadvantages which arise as a result of the absence of a statute. The difficulties include:

- what, if anything, should be excluded from a living will?
- what presumptions, if any, arise from a living will?
- how can health professionals be protected?
- for how long is an advanced refusal valid?
- how should a living will be drawn up?
- what rights, if any, should relatives have in relation to a living will?

These are discussed more fully by the author (Dimond, 2000).

Case scenario

In Mary's situation, it is clear that her advanced directive was drawn up many years before she became a victim to Alzheimer's disease. It is possible that in that time many advances in medical treatment had taken place. If staff are concerned about the validity of a living will, an application could be made to court for a declaration as to whether the living will is valid and binding. In the meantime, action could be taken to keep Mary alive until such time as the court makes its decision known. In certain circumstances, this would defeat the object of the refusal. If, for example, a Jehovah's Witness refused blood by means of an advanced statement, but there were doubts as to its validity, to keep the patient alive by blood transfusion until the validity of the direction was reviewed by the court would be nonsensical. In Mary's advanced directive, she has refused every intervention including feeding and pain relief. Is this valid? In theory, a mentally competent person can refuse every kind of treatment, including food, and it should follow that everything should be capable of being refused in advance. If Mary was mentally competent at the time that she drew up the living will, and if it is, therefore, valid, her refusal of food and pain relief should be binding on the health professionals caring for her. However, the Law Commission, in its draft bill, had recommended that a living will could not exclude the giving of basic care. This was defined as:

> *Care to maintain bodily cleanliness and to alleviate severe pain and the provision of direct oral nutrition and hydration.*

If a statute had been passed covering living wills and including this provision, the effect would have been that although patients might have included in their living will a request that they were not given pain relief, this request could have been ignored by health professionals caring for them, if they considered that it was in the best interests of the patients. In other words, a certain degree of paternalism would have been permitted.

However, certain cultures, such as Buddhism, would not wish to have sedatives or medication for pain relief. Their autonomy would be undermined by ignoring such provisions in a living will. From the perspective of the health professional, it can be appreciated that it would be very difficult to care for a patient who by a living will had refused certain basic treatments and whose condition deteriorated with severe pain, thirst and filth.

There has not, to the author's knowledge, been a case where a competent person has refused to accept pain relief or basic care. In *Re C. (adult refusal of treatment)* [1994], a Broadmoor patient had refused to have a life-saving amputation on the grounds that he would prefer to die with two legs than survive with one. The court held that the patient did have the capacity to make a valid decision; he was able to understand the information which was given to him and he was able to understand the consequences of his refusal. His refusal was therefore binding upon the doctors (see *Chapter 6* for fuller discussion of the case). If a case such as Mary's were to come before the courts, the judges would have to establish at common law a principle as to whether a mentally capable adult could refuse in advance such basic care as defined by the Law Commission. Until such a case is heard, the question must be open to doubt.

Conclusion

While the basic principle that a mentally competent person can decide in advance which treatments he/she would refuse if he/she was subsequently to become mentally incapacitated is clearly accepted at common law, there are, in the absence of statutory provisions, doubts as to the detailed rules applying to such directives. It is to be hoped that there will eventually be statutory provision since these uncertainties need to be resolved. If this country follows the pattern found in the USA, there are likely to be an increasing number of people who consider in advance how they would not wish to be treated if they become mentally incapacitated and who draw up living wills. Health professionals are increasingly likely to be confronted by issues such as those cited in this chapter.

In the next chapter we shall consider the law which relates to 'not for resuscitation' instructions.

References

Dimond B (2000) The legal aspects of living wills: a need for clarity. *Int J Palliative Care* **6**(6): 304–7

Law Commission (1995) *Mental Incapacity*. Report No 231. The Stationery Office, London

Lord Chancellor (1997) *Who Decides? Lord Chancellor's Office*. The Stationery Office, London

Lord Chancellor (1999) *Making Decisions: The Government's Proposals for Making Decisions on Behalf of Mentally Incapacitated Adults*. The Stationery Office, London

Re C. (adult refusal of treatment) [1994] 1 WLR 290

18

Not for resuscitation instructions

Box 18.1: Case scenario

Ben, aged seventy-five years, was extremely depressed following the death of his wife. He was admitted to hospital in an emergency for an appendectomy. A young doctor told the nurse that he had spoken to Ben's son and it was agreed that in the event of a cardiac arrest Ben should not be resuscitated. This instruction was not put in writing. Unfortunately, after his return to the ward from the recovery room, Ben arrested. What should the nursing staff do?

Introduction

Life and death decisions over whether or not a person is to be resuscitated, if not considered before an emergency arises, can lead to a difficult situation for nursing staff and others. In the above case scenario, a nurse who decided that Ben should be resuscitated and called out the team may be criticised by medical staff who say that the instructions were that Ben should not be resuscitated. On the other hand, if the nurse, conforming to the instructions of the junior doctor, did not call out the crash team, the consultant could subsequently criticise her on the grounds that the junior doctor had not discussed this with the medical team and there were no 'not for resuscitation' (NFR) or 'do not resuscitate' (DNR) instructions written in the notes.

Clarity of instructions based firmly on the legal principles is essential both to protect the rights of the patient and to protect the position of staff.

The patient's rights

A patient has a right to be resuscitated, if the procedure is reasonably likely to be successful and if he/she has a reasonably good prognosis following resuscitation.

European Convention on Human Rights

Under article 2 of the European Convention on Human Rights, every person has a right to life. It could be argued that failure to resuscitate in circumstances favourable to the patient is a denial of this right.

Article 2 of the European Convention of Human Rights states that:

> *Everyone's right to life shall be protected by law. No one shall be deprived of his life intentionally save in the execution of a sentence of a court following his conviction of a crime for which this penalty is provided by law.*

Recent decisions of the courts show how this right is interpreted. For example, in a recent case (*A National Health Service Trust* v. *D.*, 2000), parents lost their attempt to ensure that a severely handicapped baby born prematurely was resuscitated if necessary. The judge ruled that the hospital should provide him with palliative care to ease his suffering, but should not try to revive him as that would cause unnecessary pain.

In another case, the President of the Family Division, Dame Elizabeth Butler-Schloss, held that the withdrawal of life-sustaining medical treatment was not contrary to article 2 of the Human Rights Convention and the right to life where the patient was in a persistent vegetative state (PVS). The ruling was made on 25 October 2000 in cases involving Mrs M., a forty-nine-year-old woman, who suffered brain damage during an operation abroad in 1997 and was diagnosed as being in a PVS in October 1998, and in the case of Mrs H., aged thirty-six, who fell ill in America as a result of pancreatitis during Christmas 1999 (*NHS Trust A.* v. *Mrs M.* and *NHS Trust B.* v. *Mrs H.*) In the light of these decisions, it would appear that failure to resuscitate a patient when circumstances justify the decision would not amount to a breach of article 2.

Article 3 of the European Convention of Human Rights states that:

> *No one shall be subjected to torture or to inhuman or degrading treatment or punishment.*

Failure to resuscitate Ben when all the circumstances (likely success and good prognosis) are favourable may be defined as inhuman treatment.

Duty of care in the law of negligence

Ben is also owed a duty of care by the medical and nursing staff caring for him. The standard of care of this duty, as defined by the Bolam Test (*Bolam* v. *Friern Hospital Management Committee* [1957]), would require staff to follow a reasonable standard of care conforming to the acceptable approved practice of a competent body of professional opinion.

If, in a case such as Ben's, reasonable practice would have indicated resuscitation, then it could be argued that failure to resuscitate was a breach of the duty of care. If as a result of this failure Ben suffered harm (ie. death), then his relatives could sue in his name for breach of the duty of care owed to him.

What if Ben were able to express his own wishes?

If Ben were asked before the operation what he would wish to happen in the event of a cardiac arrest and stated that he would not wish to be resuscitated, then his wishes should prevail. Care should be taken to ensure that he has the mental capacity to make such a decision. It may be, for example, that Ben is severely depressed following the bereavement and this is affecting his thinking. His request for no resuscitation may be a result of that depression and not a competent decision.

Professionals have a duty when a person refuses what could be life-saving treatment to ensure that the person is mentally competent (*Re T. (adult: refusal of medical treatment)* [1992]; *Chapter 16*). If, however, it is clear that Ben has the necessary mental capacity and clearly indicates that he does not wish to be resuscitated then it is Ben's legal right to refuse treatment (*Re MB. (adult medical treatment)* [1997]; *Chapters 2* and *12*).

What if Ben were incompetent?

If Ben were incompetent, then staff would have to decide what was in his best interests in determining whether or not NFR instructions were appropriate. Acting in the best interests of a mentally incapacitated adult was considered in *Chapter 11*. The House of Lords has laid down the principle that health professionals have a duty in law to act out of necessity in the best interests of a mentally incapacitated adult person (*Re F. (mental patient: sterilisation)* [1990]; *Chapter 7*).

What rights do the relatives have?

In Ben's situation, his son has already told the medical staff that Ben should not be resuscitated. Relatives have no legal right to make decisions on behalf of a mentally incapacitated adult and it would be dangerous to rely upon views given by relatives unless there is clear evidence that the son is expressing Ben's wishes. In the absence of a living will (*Chapter 17*) or advance refusal of resuscitation, it is extremely uncertain what Ben wants. In this case, he has to be treated as a mentally incapacitated adult and actions taken in his best interests. It is, of course, important to discuss potential treatment plans with relatives because they may be able to shed light on the patient's views, but relatives do not have the right to make decisions in the case of a mentally incapacitated adult.

Professional guidance

Before the implementation of the Human Rights Act 1998, the Department of Health drew attention to guidance which had been drawn up by the Resuscitation Council, the Royal College of Nursing and the British Medical Association (BMA/Resuscitation Council/ RCN, 1999). (This guidance has since been updated: BMA/RCN/ Resuscitation Council (UK), 2001.) The guidance was commended to NHS trusts in September 2000 by the NHS Executive (2000) in a NHS circular.

By this circular, chief executives of NHS trusts are required to ensure that appropriate resuscitation policies which respect patients' rights are in place, understood by all relevant staff, and accessible to those who need them, and that such policies are subject to appropriate audit and monitoring arrangements. The action required to be taken by NHS trusts is shown in *Table 18.1*.

The Commission for Health Improvement (CHI) has been asked by the Secretary of State to pay particular attention to resuscitation decision-making processes as part of its rolling programme of reviews of clinical governance arrangements put in place by NHS organisations.

Guidance emphasises that there must be no blanket policies, each individual patient must be assessed personally and policy cannot depend solely on the age of the patient.

Table 18.1: Resuscitation policies: action to be taken by NHS trusts

Action to be taken by NHS trusts to ensure:

- Patients' rights are central to decision making on resuscitation
- The trust has an agreed resuscitation policy in place which respects patients' rights
- The policy is published and readily available to those who may wish to consult it, including patients, families and carers
- Appropriate arrangements are in place for ensuring that all staff who may be involved in resuscitation decisions understand and implement the policy
- Appropriate supervision arrangements are in place to review the resuscitation decisions
- Induction and staff development programmes cover the resuscitation policy
- Clinical practice in this area is regularly audited
- Clinical audit outcomes are reported in the trust's annual clinical governance report
- A non-executive director of the trust is given designated responsibility on behalf of the trust board to ensure that a resuscitation policy is agreed, implemented and regularly reviewed within the clinical governance framework

Withholding of resuscitation

According to the guidelines, cardiopulmonary resuscitation (CPR) should only be withheld in the following four situations:

- the mentally competent patient has refused treatment
- a valid living will covering such circumstances has been made by the patient
- effective CPR is unlikely to be successful
- where successful CPR is likely to be followed by a length and quality of life which would not be in the best interests of the patient to sustain.

(NHS Executive, 2000)

Box 18.2 provides a matrix showing how the factors of mental competence and prognosis impact on each other in NFR decisions.

Box 18.2: A matrix for 'not for resuscitation'

Is the patient competent?	No	Yes: patient asks for treatment	Yes: patient refuses
Good prognosis		Resuscitate	Resuscitate
Bad prognosis	NFR	???*	NFR

* Indicates a situation where the patient is asking for resuscitation and the medical view is that it would not succeed, or the prognosis of the patient is so appalling that it would not be a justification for resources to be used

A situation may arise where the patient is asking for resuscitation and the medical view is that it would not succeed or the prognosis of the patient is so appalling that it would not be a justification for resources to be used. For example, imagine that in the situation of Ben he is suffering from the final stages of cancer of the pancreas. He asks to be resuscitated, but medical staff know that he has very few days left and in his very poor state of health CPR may not succeed. In such circumstances, while Ben may want the treatment, medical staff may consider that it is unjustified. At the present time, a patient cannot insist upon treatment which would not be in accordance with the professional judgement of health staff. This also applies to parents seeking treatment for their child. In the case discussed above (*A National Health Service Trust* v. *D.*, 2000), the court held that the decision by doctors that a child should not be placed upon a ventilator was not an infringement of the child's right to life and parents could not compel the doctors to act contrary to their professional discretion.

Withholding and withdrawing life-saving treatment in children

Parents of children under eighteen years of age do have decision-making rights on behalf of the child, as long as such decisions are in the best interests of the child. Guidance has been issued by the Royal College of Paediatric and Child Health (RCPCH, 1997). The Royal College identified five situations in which withholding or withdrawing treatment may be considered:

- the brain dead child
- the permanent vegetative state
- the 'no chance' situation
- the 'no purpose' situation
- the 'unbearable' situation.

At the present time there are no clear guidelines as to when the approval of the court should be sought for withholding or withdrawing of treatment in a child and, in practice, it is probably only where there is a dispute between parents and physicians or surgeons or a third party wishes to seek a court review of what is being proposed in relation to the treatment or non-treatment of a child that an application is made to court. In the case of Re J. (1992), the baby suffered from a severe form of cerebral palsy with cortical blindness and severe epilepsy. The Court of Appeal held that the court would not exercise its inherent jurisdiction over minors by ordering a medical practitioner to treat the minor in a manner contrary to the practitioner's clinical judgement. In the practitioner's view, intensive therapeutic measures such as artificial ventilation were inappropriate. The Court of Appeal declared that it would be lawful for doctors in their professional judgement to allow a severely disabled child to die. (For further information on this subject, see Dimond, 2001: chapter 14.)

Conclusion

The recent circular from the NHS Executive should be of considerable assistance to health professional staff, who are entitled to request that any NFR instructions are in writing and that each patient is individually assessed. Such blanket policies as 'patients over eighty are not for resuscitation' are illegal. CHI has a duty to ensure that NFR policies are in place and are being implemented and this should ensure the protection of patients' rights and also the benefit of staff.

References

A National Health Service Trust v. *D.* (2000) The Times Law Report 19 July

British Medical Association, Resuscitation Council, Royal College of Nurses (1999) *Decisions Relating to Cardiopulmonary Resuscitation*. BMA, London

British Medical Association/Royal College of Nurses/Resuscitation Council (UK) (2001) *Decisions Relating to Cardiopulmonary Resuscitation. A Joint Statement from the British Medical Association, the Resuscitation Council (UK) and the Royal College of Nursing*. BMA/RCN/Resuscitation Council (UK), London

Bolam v. *Friern Hospital Management Committee* [1957] 1 WLR 582

Dimond BC (2001) *Legal Aspects of Nursing*. 3rd edn. Pearson Education, Harlow

NHS Executive (2000) Resuscitation Policy HSC 2000/028 September. NHS Executive, London

NHS Trust A. v. *Mrs M.* and *NHS Trust B.* v. *Mrs H. Family Division* The Times 25 October 2000; [2001] 1 All ER 801; [2001] 2 FLR 367

Re F. (mental patient: sterilisation) [1990] 2 AC 1

Re J. (a minor) (wardship, medical treatment) [1992] 4 All ER 614

Re MB. (adult medical treatment) [1997] 2 FLR 426

Royal College of Paediatric and Child Health (1997) *Withholding or Withdrawing Life Saving Treatment in Children; a Framework for Practice*. RCPCH, London

Re T. (adult: refusal of medical treatment) [1992] 4 All ER 649, (1992) 9 BMLR 46 CA

19

Issues relating to euthanasia

Box 19.1: Case scenario

Norah was in the terminal stages of cancer. She lived with her single daughter, Jane, and was being cared for by Macmillan nurses who came to see her daily. She was on a high level of morphine but still suffered considerable pain. A consultant in palliative care visited her to reassess her medication levels, but Norah found that the new medication still left her with considerable discomfort and pain. Norah asked her daughter to help her end her life. What is the law?

Introduction

In contrast to the Netherlands, the laws of this country make it a criminal offence to assist another person to die. According to the Suicide Act 1961 and Offences Against the Persons Act 1861, any person involved in the death of another could face the laws of murder or manslaughter. These apply even when the victim has made the request for help with full mental capacity. The consent of that individual does not constitute a defence to any of these offences. These offences will be considered in the light of Norah's situation in the above 'case scenario' (*Box 19.1*).

Murder

The definition of murder derives from a seventeenth century case:

> *Murder is when a man of sound memory, and of the age of discretion, unlawfully killeth within any country of the realm any reasonable creature in rerum natura under the King's peace, with malice aforethought, either expressed by the party or implied by law, so as the party wounded, or hurt, etc. die of the wound or hurt, etc...*

(Sir Edward Coke, 1797, cited in Dine and Gobert, 2000)

The original definition set a time limit of a year and a day in which the person must die of the wound or hurt. This limitation of time was removed in 1996. If, therefore, Norah's daughter Jane was to comply with Norah's wishes and end her life deliberately she could be found guilty of murder. In this case, at the present time, a judge has no discretion following a plea or conviction of guilty of murder, other than to sentence the accused to life imprisonment.

Manslaughter

In certain circumstances what would have been a crime of murder may be reduced to manslaughter. Manslaughter is divided into two categories: voluntary and involuntary. Voluntary covers the situation where there is the mental intention to kill or complete disregard as to the possibility that death could arise from one's actions, ie. there is the mental requirement (*mens rea*) but there are extenuating factors. For example:

- provocation
- death in pursuance of a suicide pact

- diminished responsibility.

The effect of these extenuating facts is that a murder verdict could not be obtained but the defendant could be guilty of voluntary manslaughter.

Involuntary manslaughter exists when the *mens rea* (ie. the mental element) for murder is absent. Such circumstances would include:

- gross negligence
- killing recklessly may or may not be insufficient to be murder
- an intention to escape from lawful arrest.

Defences to a charge of murder or manslaughter include:

- killing in carrying out the sentence of the court
- killing in the course of preventing crime or arresting offenders
- killing in the defence of one's own person or that of another
- killing in defence of property.

Use of excessive force will negate the defence of protecting one's own person or that of another or defending property.

Where the accused is convicted of manslaughter, the judge has complete discretion over sentencing in contrast to where there is a murder conviction.

If Norah were to be given a lethal injection by Jane, that action would probably constitute murder, but Jane may succeed in obtaining a plea of not guilty of murder but guilty of manslaughter by reason of diminished responsibility.

> **Box 19.2: The case of Dr Cox (R. v. Cox, 1992)**
>
> Lillian Boyes, an elderly patient, suffered from rheumatoid arthritis. She was in extreme pain and was terminally ill. She asked her consultant Dr Cox and others to kill her. Dr Cox administered a lethal dose of potassium chloride and she died almost immediately. He was prosecuted for attempted murder and convicted. The judge gave him a suspended prison sentence.

The case presented in *Box 19.2* is a recent case where a doctor was found guilty of manslaughter (*R.* v. *Cox*, 1992). It is noticeable that in this case Dr Cox was not charged with murder. Had he been so and found guilty of that, then the judge would have had no choice other than to impose a sentence of life imprisonment. Dr Cox also faced proceedings before the professional conduct committee of the General Medical Council and before his employers, Wessex Regional Health Authority. The case came to light because a nurse, in fulfilment of her professional duty, reported to senior management the fact that potassium chloride had been administered. Management then brought in the police. As the case of Dr Cox shows, voluntary euthanasia, by which is meant the killing of a person with that person's consent, is unlawful. The fact that the patient had pleaded with the doctor for her life to be ended was not a defence against attempted murder.

The outcome in the case of Dr Cox can be contrasted with a case where a husband killed his wife who was suffering from motor neurone disease (see *page 160*).

Assistance in a suicide bid

If the act of the person in causing a person's death amounts to assistance in a suicide bid, then it is illegal under section 2(1) of the Suicide Act 1961 which is shown in *Box 19.3*.

> **Box 19.3: Suicide Act 1961 relating to assisting a person to commit suicide**
>
> A person who aids, abets, counsels or procures the suicide of another or an attempt by another to commit suicide, shall be liable on conviction on indictment to imprisonment (up to fourteen years).

If Norah were able to end her own life without the assistance of any other person it would not be a criminal offence. Before the Suicide Act 1961, any person who attempted to commit suicide and failed could be prosecuted for the attempt to take their own life (of course, if they succeeded, they were beyond the reach of the laws of this country). The Suicide Act 1961 made it no longer a criminal offence to attempt to commit suicide, but retained the criminal offences of aiding and abetting another person's suicide.

The situation is, therefore, that if Norah succeeds in taking her own life without the involvement of any other person, then no crime has been committed. Yet, if Jane helps her in any way at all — and it will be noted that the words 'aids', 'abets', 'counsels', 'procures' or 'attempts' any such action are extremely wide, then such help would constitute an offence under the Suicide Act 1961. The words used in the Act would cover Jane obtaining a publication giving advice on suicide, or leaving tablets by Norah's bed, if she knew that Norah wanted to take her own life, and any other form of encouragement or assistance by Jane.

Letting die and killing

While assisting a person to die is illegal in this country, it may in certain circumstances be lawful to allow a person to die, ie. to let nature take its course. This could arise where either a mentally capacitated person had refused treatment or it was considered to be in the best interests of the person to be allowed to die.

The Tony Bland case (*Airedale NHS Trust* v. *Bland* [1993]) is an example where the House of Lords held that it was in the best interests of this person who was in a persistent vegetative state to be allowed to die and for the artificial feeding to cease. Where the patient has the necessary mental capacity, then he/she is entitled to refuse life-saving treatment. Thus, Norah could refuse any further treatment in the hope that she would die quicker.

Treatment which reduces life expectancy

Since Norah is in extreme pain it may be necessary to increase her level of morphine to such a point that the medication will actually reduce her life expectancy. However, if the intention is to control her pain and not to bring about her death and the level of medication is in accordance with reasonable medical practice, then giving her medication would not constitute a criminal offence of murder or manslaughter. The dose level would have to accord with the Bolam Test (*Bolam* v. *Friern Hospital Management Committee* [1957]) as to what is reasonable practice.

This issue arose in the trial of Dr Bodkin Adams who was charged with the murder of an elderly woman who was receiving twenty-four-hour nursing care in Eastbourne by giving her excessive amounts of morphine (*R.* v. *Adams (Bodkin)* [1957]). The trial judge made it clear to the jury that a doctor has a duty to care for a dying patient and is able to ensure that the patient is given appropriate pain relief, even if the effect of the medication is to reduce the life expectancy of the patient. If, however, the doctor administered medication with the intention of reducing the life of the patient that would be unlawful.

The Netherlands

Several countries have brought in legislation to decriminalise voluntary euthanasia, so that a mentally competent person who is dying can have assistance in ending his/her life, which is recognised as lawful. In the Netherlands (Battin, 1992), for example, a doctor will not be prosecuted if he/she has assisted a dying person to die, provided that the doctor has followed specific requirements, including obtaining the written consent of a mentally capacitated patient.

The House of Lords

The House of Lords in a Select Committee report (House of Lords Select Committee on Medical Ethics, 1993–1994) has strongly advocated against any relaxation of the laws which would permit voluntary euthanasia in the UK. This has also been the stance of the Government in its White Paper on decision making on behalf of mentally incapacitated adults (Lord Chancellor, 1999).

The case of Diane Pretty (*R. (On the application of Pretty)* v. *DPP* [2001])

In a recent well-publicised case, Diane Pretty, a sufferer of motor neurone disease, appealed to the House of Lords that her husband should be allowed to end her life, and not be prosecuted under the Suicide Act 1961. The House of Lords did not allow her appeal. It held that if there were to be any changes to the Suicide Act to legalise the killing of another person, then these changes should be made by Parliament.

As the law stood, the Suicide Act made it a criminal offence to aid and abet the suicide of another person and the husband could not be granted an immunity from prosecution were he to assist his wife to die. The House of Lords held that there was no conflict between the human rights of Mrs Pretty as set out in the European Convention on Human Rights (*Chapter 2*). Mrs Pretty then applied to the European Court of Human Rights in Strasbourg, but the European Court of Human Rights did not find in her favour.

It held that there was no conflict between the Suicide Act 1961 and the European Convention of Human Rights. The Council of Europe issued a press release entitled Chamber judgement in the case of *Pretty* v. *the United Kingdom* published on April 29 2002. It stated that the European Court of Human Rights has refused an application by Diane Pretty, a British national dying of motor neurone disease, for a ruling that would allow her husband to assist her to commit suicide without facing prosecution under the Suicide Act 1961 section 2(1). The applicant is paralysed from the neck downwards and has a poor life expectancy, while her intellect and decision-making capacity remain unimpaired. She wanted to be given the right to decide when and how she died without undergoing further suffering and indignity. The court unanimously found the application inadmissible with no violations under the European Convention of Human Rights under: Article 2 the right to life; Article 3 prohibition of human or degrading treatment or punishment; Article 8 the right to respect for private life; Article 9 freedom of conscience and Article 14 prohibition of discrimination.

It was subsequently reported that Diane Pretty had died.

Mercy killing

Even though the law treats voluntary euthanasia as a criminal offence, the actual punishment given to offenders depends upon the attitude taken by the judge in sentencing. A conviction for murder, as was noted above, is followed by life imprisonment; the judge has no discretion. There have been cases where a person found guilty of manslaughter in a mercy killing situation has been given a non-custodial sentence. For example, in a recent case (Peek, 2002), Mr Lionel Bailey the husband of a woman suffering from motor neurone disease smothered his wife with a pillow, to release her from pain. He pleaded guilty to manslaughter on the grounds of diminished responsibility. A plea of not guilty to murder was accepted by the prosecution. The judge sentenced him to a three-year community rehabilitation order. The judge said that

In my view, the interests of justice do not require me to impose a custodial sentence in this case. I accept that the strain you were under watching a much-loved wife deteriorate due to the cruelty of illness must have been well-nigh unbearable. You were in your seventies, in poor health, and yet continued to do your loving best to care for her as a loyal husband should. That anguish must have been intense. You couldn't bear to see her suffering any longer. I'm sure you did what you did to end her suffering without a thought for yourself and I make that quite plain.

Some have argued that in the light of such judgements, the law should be amended to recognise voluntary euthanasia as lawful. However, it does not follow that because in some cases, the perpetrators of mercy killing are treated leniently that the law recognises such actions as justified. They are still criminal offences and an offender cannot be sure how he or she will be treated by the courts.

Conclusion

At present the law is clear: health professionals cannot deliberately shorten the lives of their patients or assist them in a suicide attempt. They must respect the wishes of their mentally capacitated patients to refuse treatment and where patients lack the mental capacity and their prognosis is appalling or they are in a situation such as persistent vegetative state, then they can, if it is in their best interests, be allowed to die. However, there are clear advantages in seeking the views of the court in the latter circumstances and in the case of patients in a persistent vegetative state (PVS), a Practice Direction (Practice Note [1996]) was issued by the courts requiring a court declaration to be sought before any life-saving procedures can be withdrawn. Subsequently, new guidance has been issued which incorporates this 1996 guidance as well as guidance on sterilisation of mentally incapacitated adults (*Chapter 7*) (Practice Note [2001]). For decisions relating to the withholding or withdrawing of treatment in children see *Chapter 18*.

References

Airedale NHS Trust v. *Bland* [1993] 1 All ER 821

Battin M (1992) Voluntary euthanasia and the risk of abuse: can we learn anything from the Netherlands. *Law Med Health Care* **20**(1–2): 133–43

Bolam v. *Friern Hospital Management Committee* [1957] 2 All ER 118

Dine J, Gobert J (2000) *Cases and Materials on Criminal Law*. 3rd edn. Blackstone Press, London

House of Lords Select Committee on Medical Ethics (1993–1994) HL Paper 21, House of Lords Select Committee on Medical Ethics, London

Lord Chancellor (1999) *Making Decisions: The Government's Proposals for Making Decisions on Behalf of Mentally Incapacitated Adults*. The Stationery Office, London

Peek L (2002) Mercy for husband who killed wife in pain. *The Times*, 7 September

Practice Note [1996] (Official Solicitor to the Supreme Court: Vegetative State); [1996] 4 All ER 766; [1996] 2 FLR 375

Practice Note [2001] (Official Solicitor: Declaratory Proceedings: Medical and Welfare Proceedings for Adults who lack Capacity) [2001] 2 FLR 158; [2001] 2 FCR 94

Pretty v. *United Kingdom ECHR* the full judgement is available on: http://www.echr.coe.int/Eng/Press/apr/Prettyjndepress.htm. (Current Law 380 June 2002)

R. (on the application of Pretty) v. *DPP* [2001] UKHL 61, [2001] 3 WLR 1598

R. v. *Cox (1992)* 12 BMLR 38. Winchester Crown Court

R. v. *Adams (Bodkin)* [1957] Crim LR 365

20

Research and the mentally competent adult

Box 20.1: Case scenario

Sylvia was admitted to hospital for a hysterectomy. Before the operation, she agreed to take part in a research project designed to test the effectiveness of different forms of operative care, and understood that some additional tissue would be removed. The day after the operation she suffered from extreme pain and felt sure that this was because of the additional procedure undertaken. She now regrets agreeing to participate in the research and is wondering what action she can take. What is the law?

Introduction

Research-based, clinically effective practice is becoming part of the reasonable standard of care, and over the next few years there will be increasing pressure to ensure that every activity, task, and item of care and treatment by all health professionals is subjected to scientific analysis as to its effectiveness. Research activities will become an increasingly important part of health care, and there is additional pressure for those who use complementary or alternative therapies to prove that these are effective.

Nursing staff will increasingly find that they are caring for patients who are research subjects. In addition, nurses will have to keep abreast of research findings to ensure that their professional practice accords with approved clinically effective practice. For example, the National Institute for Clinical Excellence (NICE), through its publications, promotes research-based practice.

In this chapter we consider the law which applies to research involving mentally competent adults. The next chapter examines issues relating to children and mentally incapacitated adults in the context of the law on consent.

Principles of consent to research participation

To be valid, consent to participation in research by mentally competent people must be given voluntarily, without coercion or deceit, and in the light of information about the risks of significant harm arising from the research. People should have the right to withdraw from the research when they wish (this, however, would be subject to ensuring that they did not suffer as a result of the withdrawal). They should not suffer any discrimination as a result of their wish to withdraw from, or refuse to participate in, the research. These basic principles are recognised by case law (ie. common law, judge-made law) in this country. There is, however, no legislation setting out the rights of subjects in research projects. There are several international codes or conventions which are recognised by professional organisations in this country, but these codes have not been incorporated into the laws of this country, unlike the European Convention on Human Rights, which came into force in England, Wales and Northern Ireland on 2 October 2000 and in Scotland on devolution.

International Conventions

Nuremberg Code

At the end of the Second World War, military trials were held in Nuremberg where some of the worst perpetrators of crimes against humanity in the Nazi party were prosecuted. In its judgement, the court set out two basic principles which should be observed in order to satisfy moral, ethical and legal concepts. These have become known as the Nuremberg Code (Kennedy and Grubb, 2000) (*Table 20.1*).

Declaration of Helsinki

The World Medical Association published a Declaration of Helsinki in 1964 which set out principles for the carrying out of research on human subjects. Amendments were made in 2000 following a conference in Edinburgh (European Forum for Good Clinical Practice, 1999). The principle clauses in this declaration relating to consent are shown in *Table 20.2*.

Table 20.1: Research principles from the Nuremberg Code

- The voluntary consent of the human subject is absolutely essential

- The experiment should be such as to yield fruitful results for the good of society, unprocurable by other methods

- The experiment should be based on results of animal experiments and a knowledge of the natural history of the disease or other problem so that the anticipated results should justify the performance of the experiment

- The experiment should be so conducted as to avoid all unnecessary physical and mental suffering and injury

- No experiment should be conducted where there is an *a priori* reason to believe that death or disabling injury will occur; except, perhaps, in those circumstances where the experimental physicians also serve as subjects

- The degree of risk to be taken should never exceed that determined by the humanitarian importance of the problem to be solved by the experiment

- Proper preparations should be made and adequate facilities provided to protect the experimental subject against even remote possibilities of injury, disability or death

- The experiment should be conducted only by a scientifically qualified person

- The highest degree of skill and care should be required through all stages of the experiment of those who conduct or engage in the experiment

- During the course of the experiment the human subject should be at liberty to bring the experiment to an end if he has reached the physical or mental state where continuation of the experiment seems to him to be impossible

- During the course of the experiment the scientist in charge must be prepared to terminate the experiment at any stage, if he has probable cause to believe, in the exercise of the good faith, superior skill and careful judgement required of him that a continuation of the experiment is likely to result in injury, disability, or death to the experimental subject

Source: http://www.ushmm.org/research/doctors/Nuremberg_Code.htm

Table 20.2: Clauses in the Declaration of Helsinki relating to research

5. In medical research on human subjects, considerations related to the well-being of the human subject should take precedence over the interests of science and society

6. The primary purpose of medical research involving human subjects is to improve prophylactic, diagnostic and therapeutic procedures and the understanding of the aetiology and pathogenesis of disease. Even the best proven prophylactic, diagnostic, and therapeutic methods must continuously be challenged through research for their effectiveness, efficiency, accessibility and quality

7. In current medical practice and in medical research, most prophylactic, diagnostic and therapeutic procedures involve risks and burdens

8. Medical research is subject to ethical standards that promote respect for all human beings and protect their health and rights. Some research populations are vulnerable and need special protection. The particular needs of the economically and medically disadvantaged must be recognised. Special attention is also required for those who cannot give or refuse consent for themselves, for those who may be subject to giving consent under duress, for those who will not benefit personally from the research and for those for whom the research is combined with care

9. Research investigators should be aware of the ethical, legal and regulatory requirements for research on human subjects in their own countries as well as applicable international requirements. No national, ethical, legal or regulatory requirement should be allowed to reduce or eliminate any of the protections for human subjects set forth in this Declaration

Convention on human rights and biomedicine

A Convention for the protection of human rights and dignity of the human being with regard to the application of biology and medicine: Convention on human rights and biomedicine (Council of Europe, 1997) also sets principles for the conduct of research.

Local research ethics committees (LRECs)

The Department of Health has requested each health authority to ensure that an LREC is set up to examine research proposals (Local Research Ethics Committees, 1991). Any NHS body asked to agree a research proposal falling within its sphere of responsibility should ensure that it has been submitted to the appropriate LREC for research ethics approval. Guidance is provided on every aspect of its work, including the special procedure for multicentre research (King's College, 1997).

In certain cases, multicentre research ethics committees (MRECs), established by the Department of Health, oversee research which is carried on across several LREC catchment areas. Where less than five LRECs are involved, one LREC can act on behalf of the others. The role of the LREC is defined as being: 'To consider the ethics of proposed research projects which will involve human subjects and to advise the NHS body concerned' (DoH, 1991).

The LREC comprises multidisciplinary members including lay persons. The Royal College of Physicians published guidelines on the practice of ethics committees (Royal College of Physicians, 1996). Every research project involving patients or their records must be approved by an LREC. The LREC will look at the assessment of risks, if any, to all participants. It will also consider the consent form, the written information given to the patient about the research and ensure that there is justification for the research taking place. Any health professional who is caring for patients who are involved in a research project would be entitled to see evidence of LREC approval.

How much information should be given to data subjects?

There is justification for believing that people who volunteer for research projects as healthy volunteers who have no immediate benefit from the research should be given more information about any potential risks than a patient who stands to benefit personally from the treatment which is the subject of the research. Such a presumption is based on a distinction between therapeutic and non-therapeutic research. This distinction was recognised in the Helsinki Declaration (ie. research which is linked with the treatment of the patient being described as 'therapeutic', whereas research which has no immediate benefit to that particular patient being described as 'non-therapeutic').

However, in the discussions which took place between 1998 and 2000 on revisions to the Declaration of Helsinki it was agreed that the distinction should be dropped from the Declaration. However, in practice the distinction may be important, particularly in the care of children and mentally incapacitated adults, where therapeutic research may be justified in their best interests (see *Chapter 21*).

The principles set out by the House of Lords in the case of *Sidaway* v. *Bethlem Royal Hospital Governors* [1985] would apply to the giving of information to the subject in a research project, ie. that the researcher should follow the reasonably accepted practice. However, it could be argued that where a healthy volunteer is offering his/her services, there is no room for the therapeutic privilege of withholding information from the person. The volunteer is entitled to all information about the project. It could also be argued that in the case of the healthy volunteer participating in non-therapeutic research, there would be a duty in law for the research to pass on every item of information available to him/her which might affect participation in the research or which might be asked for by the research subject. The General Medical Council (1998) advises its registered members to be sure that anyone asked to take part in the research is given the fullest possible information, presented in terms and in a form that they can understand.

What is meant by voluntary?

> **Box 20.2: Inducement to participate in research**
>
> Brenda is a single mother dependent on income from social security. She has three children and finds it difficult to manage financially, being over £500 in debt. A local pharmaceutical company is advertising for volunteers for their drug testing programme and offering up to £1000 as inconvenience payments. Brenda decides to volunteer. What is the law?

In relation to the scenario outlined in *Box 20.2*, while the pharmaceutical company might consider that £1000 is pin money and unlikely to be an inducement, from Brenda's perspective such wealth and the opportunity to clear her debts is a significant attraction. To what extent can it be said that Brenda has voluntarily consented to the research? According to the Department of Health Local Research Ethics Committees (1991) guidance:

> *Payment in cash or kind to volunteers should only be for expense, time and inconvenience reasonably incurred.*

Whether a person is truly a volunteer is a question of the fact of each case. On the facts it would seem that the assessment of the cost of inconvenience in Brenda's case is not related to her economic circumstances. The difficulty is that Brenda may still be prepared to be a volunteer for half or even a quarter of that payment. Perhaps people in Brenda's situation should not be seen as potential volunteers. One could conclude that, in law, Brenda gave full consent to participation in the research, but that the ethical principles laid down in the international codes requiring no inducement have been broken.

Harm suffered by the research subject

The main remedies in law for failures by the researcher are:

- ❖ Trespass to the person if consent has been obtained by fraud or duress.
- ❖ An action for negligence if there has been a failure to fulfil the duty of care in relation to the safety of the research subject or if there has been a failure to provide reasonable information about the risks which could arise from the research.

Turning to the plight of Sylvia as outlined in *Box 20.1*, there is no clear evidence that the pain she is suffering from is the result of the research or pain she would have had anyway from that type of operation. At present there is no system of strict liability for those undertaking research. To obtain compensation, Sylvia would have to show, like any other patient claiming compensation for negligence, that she was owed a duty of care, that there was a failure to follow the reasonable standard of care and as a reasonably foreseeable consequence she has suffered harm.

The Royal Commission Report chaired by Lord Pearson (1978) recommended that both volunteers and patients who take part in medical research and clinical trials and who suffer severe damage as a result should receive compensation on the basis of strict liability. This recommendation has never been implemented in law, although the Association of British Pharmaceutical Industry has recommended that such persons should obtain compensation without proof of negligence if harm arose as a result of the research project.

Research ethics committees are required to establish that there has been an agreement to pay compensation before any research on medicinal products takes place. In Sylvia's case it would not appear that a pharmaceutical company is involved, so she would have to pursue a remedy through the courts, with a very dubious chance of success.

Full and informed consent

If we really wish to ensure that volunteers and participants in research projects are really informed, then there is much to be said for requiring the same high standards of consent, which are required of those prepared to donate an organ when the person is not genetically related to the recipient (*Chapter 14*). Here specific conditions of consent are required by law (The Human Organ Transplants, 1989). Adapting these for the purpose of consent to research we would have the conditions shown in *Table 20.3*.

Researchers may well protest that there is considerable difference between a living person donating an organ to someone who is not genetically related and a mentally competent person participating in a research project. However, statutory conditions of consent with an external person verifying this might well be justified in the interests of research subjects.

Table 20.3: Suggested conditions for giving consent to participation in a research project

a. That a registered medical practitioner has given the potential research subject an explanation of the nature of the medical procedure for, and the risk involved in, the research in question

b. That the potential research subject understands the nature of the medical procedure and the risks, as explained by the registered medical practitioner, and consents to participation in the research in question

c. That the potential research subject's consent to the participation in the research in question was not obtained by coercion or the offer of an inducement

d. That the potential research subject understands that he is entitled to withdraw his consent if he wishes, but has not done so

e. That the potential research subject and the researcher have both been interviewed by a person who appears to the authority to have been suitably qualified to conduct such interviews and who has reported to the authority on the conditions contained in subparagraphs a–d above and has included in his report an account of any difficulties of communication with the potential research subject or the researcher and an explanation of how those difficulties were overcome

Conclusion

Local research ethics committees have a considerable responsibility in ensuring that all research involving patients complies with the law and ethical principles. There would now seem to be justification for legislation to implement the recommendations of the Lord Pearson (1978) report that any person suffering harm during a research project should obtain compensation on the basis of strict liability. In the next chapter we consider the law as it applies to children and mentally incapacitated adults taking part in research.

References

Council of Europe (1997) Convention for the Protection of Human Rights and Dignity of the Human Being with Regard to the Application of Biology and Medicine. 4.iv. Council of Europe

Department of Health (1991) *Local Research Ethics Committees*. HSG(91)5. DoH, London

European Forum for Good Clinical Practice (1999) Bulletin of Medical Ethics: Revising the Declaration of Helsinki: A Fresh Start. *Bulletin of Medical Ethics*, London

General Medical Council (1998) *Seeking Patients' Consent: The Ethical Considerations*. General Medical Council, London

Kennedy I, Grubb A (2000) *Medical Law*. 3rd edn. Butterworths, London

King's College (1997) *Manual for Research Ethics Committees*. Centre for Medical Law and Ethics, King's College, London

Lord Pearson (1978) Royal Commission on Civil Liability and Compensation for Personal Injury. Chaired by Lord Pearson. Cmnd 7054. HMSO, London

Royal College of Physicians (1996) *Guidelines on the Practice of Ethics Committees in Medical Research Involving Human Subjects*. 3rd edn. Royal College of Physicians, London

Sidaway v. *Bethlem Royal Hospital Governors* [1985] 1 All ER 643, [1985] AC 871

The Human Organ Transplants (1989) (Unrelated persons) Regulations 1989 SI 2480. Statutory Instrument. The Stationery Office, London

21

Research using children or mentally incapable adults

> **Box 21.1: Case scenario**
>
> James is ten years old and is suffering from leukaemia. He has had a bone marrow transplant which at first appeared to succeed, but has now failed. The health authority has refused, in the best interests of James, to fund further chemotherapy and a second bone marrow transplant. However, the pioneer of a new treatment for leukaemia has offered to provide treatment for James without any cost to the family. The family is tempted by the possibility of James' life being saved. What is the law?

Introduction

In the last chapter, the basic principles of law which applied to consent by mentally capable adults in research projects were considered. In this chapter we examine the law relating to children and mentally incapable adults and their participation in research projects. It was noted in the previous chapter that there is no statutory scheme for research participation, but several international codes or conventions are recognised by professional associations in this country. These also apply to research participation by children and mentally incapacitated adults. In addition, the United Nations' *Convention on the Rights of the Child* protects the rights of the child (United Nations, 1989).

Where patients lack the capacity to make their own decisions, it is considered that different principles arise depending on whether or not the research has therapeutic benefits for the research subject. Thus, although this distinction has been abandoned in the revisions to the Declaration of Helsinki (*Chapter 20*), it is submitted that it still has a place where the care of those lacking mental capacity is considered.

Children

The United Nations' *Convention on the Rights of the Child* and profession guidance

The 1989 United Nations' *Convention on the Rights of the Child* represents clear guidance for the development of rights-based and child-centred health care. The UK ratified the Convention in 1991. Most health professional organisations have produced guidelines in respect of different aspects of research along the lines of the international conventions. Thus, the Royal College of Paediatrics and Child Health (in its previous identity of the British Paediatric Association) provided a guide to the UN Convention (British Paediatric Association, 1995). Subsequently, the Royal College of Paediatrics and Child Health has published guidelines on clinical research involving newborn babies and infants (Royal College of Paediatrics and Child Health, 1999) and children (Royal College of Paediatrics and Child Health, 2000).

Therapeutic research

Statutory right of the sixteen- and seventeen-year-olds

Under section 8(1) of the Family Law Reform Act 1969, a young person of sixteen or seventeen can give a valid consent to medical, dental and surgical treatment (*Chapter 8*). Treatment is defined in section 8(2) as including:

> ... *any procedure undertaken for the purposes of diagnosis*

> *and this section applies to any procedures (including, in particular, the administration of an anaesthetic) which is ancillary to any treatment as it applies to that treatment.*

(Family Law Reform Act 1969, section 8(1))

There is no mention of participation in research in this definition, so it could be assumed that a young person of sixteen or seventeen does not have a statutory right to participate in non-therapeutic research as a healthy volunteer. However, this right might exist at common law (see below), but there could be circumstances where the research is such an integral part of the treatment, ie. the treatment would proceed anyway, but the researchers want to compare this patient group with another on a different treatment. In this case, it could be argued that there would be a statutory right under section 8(1). It all depends upon the ratio of treatment to research in the aims of the health professional.

Common law powers of child to give consent to participation in research

If the statutory right does not apply, then under the Gillick principles (*Gillick* v. *W. Norfolk and Wisbech Area Health Authority* [1986]) a youngster of sixteen and seventeen years may have the mental capacity to give a valid consent to participation in the research project. So also may a child under that age, but clearly the test of competence must cover the capacity to understand any potential risks arising from the research project.

Common law powers of the parents to give consent

If the child stands to benefit from participation in the research, then it is probable that parents could give consent on the child's behalf, providing that such participation was in the child's best interests. This is only likely to apply if the research is therapeutic and part of a treatment plan for that child. If, however, there are recognised existing treatments which work, then it could be argued that participation in unknown treatments carry a risk to which the parent could not give consent on the child's behalf.

Looking at the situation in *Box 21.1*, it could be argued that the existing treatments have failed, and the parents could give consent on James' behalf to participation in this new pioneering treatment. However, there are many unanswered questions:

- is James likely to suffer pain and discomfort in participating?
- do the benefits of the possible success outweigh the risks of harm?
- since the welfare of James is the paramount consideration, would any court justify participation in his best interests?

If the health authority had decided against funding more treatment in his best interests, it could apply for James to be made a ward of court, so that the court could decide if it was in the best interests of James for him to participate in the research.

Non-therapeutic research and children

It could be argued that parents have no right to make any decision which is not in the best interests of their children. It would therefore follow that they could not give consent to the child's participation in research as a healthy volunteer whatever the level of risk. In a sense this is to deny a child the right of being altruistic. Only if a child was Gillick competent according to the level of competence required for participation in a research project and gave an informed and entirely voluntary consent, could a child participate as a healthy volunteer. In practice this rigid rule is not followed and provided that there is no or only minimal risk to the child, parental consent can be given.

Mentally incapacitated adults

Therapeutic research

At present there are no statutory provisions relating to the decision making on behalf of mentally incapacitated adults (*Chapter 7*). There is, however, a common law power to act in their best interests (*Re F. (mental patient: sterilisation)* [1990]). If participation was considered to be in the best interests of a mentally incapacitated adult, then a person caring for him/her could, by acting in his/her best interests, enable that person to take part in the research project. Specific approval to the inclusion of mentally incapable adults should be obtained from the local research ethics committee (LREC).

> ### Box 21.2: Improved memory: case scenario
>
> A psychologist was researching into hemisphere function of the human brain and linked up with a pharmaceutical company which was researching into preparations which appeared to reduce memory loss. The psychologist approached a psychiatrist to inquire if he would be prepared to permit, as part of their treatment plan, those patients suffering from Alzheimer's disease to participate in this research as part of a randomly controlled test. What is the law?

A possible scenario is shown in *Box 21.2*. In this scenario, there would have to be clear analysis of any potential risks to the patients together with potential benefits and the full facts would have to be given to the LREC. (In practice, this is likely to be a multicentred research project so would be scrutinised by a multicentred research ethics committee.) It would have to be shown that it was in the best interests of each individual patient to have this treatment.

Relatives who do not have the legal right to give or withhold consent to treatment which is in the best interests of a mentally incapacitated adult, may wish to apply to the court for a declaration to be made that it is in the best interests of the mentally incapable adult.

Non-therapeutic research

In contrast to therapeutic research, it could be argued that the participation of mentally incapable adults in research from which they will never benefit can never be in their best interests and that they should be protected from such activities. There is at present no statute in England, Wales and Northern Ireland covering the situation (for Scotland see the Adults with Incapacity (Scotland) Act 2000; *Chapter 7*) but the Law Commission (Law Commission, 1995) has made recommendations for legislation, suggesting that participation of mentally incapacitated adults in non-therapeutic research could take place but on the basis of very strict criteria. It recommended the establishment of a Mental Incapacity Research Committee which should have the power to approve research if:

❖ It is desirable to provide knowledge of the causes or treatment of, or of the care of people affected by, the incapacitating condition with which any participant is or may be affected.

❖ The object of the research cannot be effectively achieved without the participation of persons who are or may be without capacity to consent.

❖ The research will not expose a participant to more than a negligible risk, will not be unduly invasive or restrictive or a participant, and will not unduly interfere with a participant's freedom of action or privacy.

❖ The Law Commission recommended that in addition to approval by the Mental Incapacity Research Committee, non-therapeutic research in relation to a person without capacity should require the approval of the court, or the consent of an attorney or manager, or a certificate by a doctor not involved in the research that the participation of the person is appropriate, or designation that the research does not involve direct contact.

Conclusion

Children and mentally incapacitated adults need statutory protection against exploitation. While the former are protected by the Children Act 1989 (but only if a person challenges proposed treatment or research) there are no statutory provisions in England, Wales and Northern Ireland for the protection of mentally incapacitated adults. There are strong arguments for ensuring the implementation of the Law Commission's proposals in law as soon as possible. Since April 2002 Scotland has had the benefit of the Adults with Incapacity (Scotland) Act 2000 (*Chapter 7*).

References

British Paediatric Association (1995) *A Paediatrician's Brief Guide to the UN Convention on the Rights of the Child.* British Paediatric Association, London

Gillick v. *W. Norfolk and Wisbech Area Health Authority* [1986] 1 AC 112

Law Commission (1995) *Mental Incapacity.* Report No 231. HMSO, London

Re F. (mental patient: sterilisation) [1990] 2 AC 1

Royal College of Paediatrics and Child Health (1999) *Safeguarding Informed Parental Involvement in Clinical Research Involving Newborn Babies and Infants.* Royal College of Paediatrics and Child Health, London

Royal College of Paediatrics and Child Health (2000) Guidelines for the ethical conduct of medical research involving children. *Arch Dis Child* **82**: 1777–82

United Nations (1989) *Convention on the Rights of the Child.* United Nations. Online at: http://www.unhchr.ch/ html/menu3/b/k2crc.htm

Amputations of healthy limbs

Introduction

The condition of body dysmorphic disorder came to light when publicity was given to a surgeon who had removed the healthy limbs of some patients (Gillian, 2000). One patient, a social worker, stated that she had fantasised about losing both her legs from the age of six years. She sought out disabled people wanting to learn about the realities of the condition. She often pretended to be disabled, and was considering having both legs amputated. A man of seventy-five years from Florida could not find a doctor to help him and shot his knee, leaving it so badly mutilated that the hospital had to amputate the leg.

In February 2000, Robert Smith, a consultant orthopaedic surgeon at Falkirk and District Royal Infirmary, removed one lower leg from each of two private patients, one from England and the other from Germany. He is reported as saying:

> *It took me eighteen months to pluck up the courage, but it was the most satisfactory operation I have ever performed. The patients were well informed about their condition, and they were the most grateful patients I have ever dealt with.*

Mr Smith also explained that his two patients had had a course of antipsychotic drugs, to which they had failed to respond, had received psychological counselling and a psychiatric assessment before surgery. From Mr Smith's perspective, he clearly believed that there was clinical justification for the operations and the patients were undoubtedly satisfied. The hospital subsequently announced that it was banning any further such amputations after a report by its ethical issues subcommittee.

The law: the patient

In theory, it could be argued that a mentally competent adult could give consent to any action upon him/her, provided that it was voluntary, and that no fraud, deceit, or compulsion had been involved. However, in a criminal case where sadomasochists were prosecuted for inflicting serious bodily harm on each other, the House of Lords refused to allow a defence of consent to the acts to prevail (*R.* v. *Brown* [1993]). However, the House of Lords stated that surgical or medical treatment is justified in law providing it is consented to or is otherwise justified in law.

Clearly, if consent is lacking then surgical or medical intervention would constitute both the criminal offence of assault and battery, or the offence of inflicting grievous bodily harm. It may also constitute the crime of maim, an old offence of causing an injury which disables a person. Treatment without consent would also constitute the civil wrong of trespass to the person.

What has not been decided by the House of Lords is whether the consent of a patient to an operation which others would see as clinically unacceptable would be sufficient to protect the surgeon from a criminal prosecution. Clearly, consent to an operation which is accepted as reasonable professional practice is very different from consent to an operation which is not supported by reasonable professional opinion.

Law Commission recommendations

The Law Commission (1995) recommended that consent in criminal law should be on a statutory basis and that there should be a clear statutory exception for medical treatment. It recommended that a person should not be guilty of an offence, notwithstanding that he/she causes injury to another of whatever degree of seriousness, if such injury is caused during the course of proper medical treatment or care administered with the consent of that other person.

It proposed that proper medical treatment should include procedures taken for the purposes of diagnosis, the prevention of disease, and the prevention of pregnancy. It lists specific procedures which should be included, ie. sterilisations, transsexual operations, abortions, operations for cosmetic purposes and procedures for the donation of regenerative tissue or non-regenerative tissue not essential for life. However, neither the general definition of medical treatment or care nor the specific examples given could be interpreted as including the amputation of healthy limbs, unless such an operation was supported by reasonable professional opinion.

The Law Commission's recommendations have not been incorporated in statute law. Even if they were to be, there is no certainty that a surgeon who performed the amputation of healthy limbs would be protected from prosecution.

Case scenario

In the case scenario presented at the beginning of this chapter, if Mr Walker carried out a procedure which does not have the support of reasonable professional practice, then he would face certain consequences in law:

- criminal prosecution for battery and criminal assault
- professional conduct proceedings by the General Medical Council (GMC)
- Disciplinary proceedings by his employer.

Criminal prosecution for battery and criminal assault

The patient's consent is the main defence against an action for trespass to the person. If the treatment is not clinically justified, in the event of the surgeon being prosecuted for criminal assault, as a result of the House of Lords' decision in the case of *R.* v. *Brown* [1993] he could probably not use successfully the fact that the patient had consented as a defence to the criminal charge.

Professional conduct proceedings by the GMC

Mr Walker also faces professional conduct proceedings by the GMC. Crucial to the determination of the proceedings would be the extent of reasonable professional opinion which supported the surgeon's actions. Also vital to its decision would be the nature of the patient's consent and the extent to which the patient had received full information about the surgery and had thoroughly explored all other treatment options before agreeing to the surgery of her healthy limbs.

Disciplinary proceedings by his employer

In the case scenario it is not clear if Mr Walker carried out the operation as part of his private practice or as an employee, so both situations will be considered.

- ❖ If Mr Walker undertook the operation privately he may still face disciplinary proceedings from any employer. An employer's disciplinary machinery is not confined to actions undertaken during the course of employment. For example, a nurse found guilty of shop-lifting could face disciplinary action from his/her employer and may lose his/her job (and also face professional conduct proceedings, as a result of which he/she could be struck off the register). If there is a nexus between unacceptable actions of an employee outside of the course of employment, then the employer would be justified in holding disciplinary proceedings. In addition, the hospital can make it clear that no such operations are to take place on its premises even though they are conducted as part of private practice. (If the surgeon works full-time in private practice then there is no employer so there would be no disciplinary proceedings.)
- ❖ If Mr Walker conducted the operation as an employee, then he could be disciplined by the employer for carrying out unacceptable surgery.

Acceptable clinical practice

The key issue is whether the actions of the surgeon are acceptable clinical practice. Research is clearly necessary on this condition and clear statements necessary from the Royal College of Psychiatry on whether there is the research evidence which would lead it to support surgery for this mental condition.

Social revulsion

Such an operation naturally results in considerable disgust. It seems to make a mockery of those who are disabled, through no fault of their own, who have to cope with missing limbs, wheelchairs and considerable restrictions on their lifestyle. The view is also held on why more is not done for the patients on a psychological level. They are clearly suffering from a major psychiatric disorder and to treat this by such drastic physical means seems quite wrong. More should be done to help them psychologically, before there is a resort to amputation.

There are other treatments and operations which are religious and cultural requirements in certain societies but which the West finds unacceptable. For example, female circumcision is a criminal offence under the Prohibition of Female Circumcision Act 1985. Guidance has been issued by the Royal College of Nursing (RCN) and British Medical Association (BMA) (RCN, 1998; BMA, 2001) to practitioners, but there is evidence that female circumcision is taking place in this country (Charter and Kennedy, 2001).

Other mutilations may also take place, such as the insertion of needles and other objects in all manner of places, but there is no specific statute law outlawing such invasions of the body. The usual laws of consent would apply.

Public policy

Public policy has to find a way between the criminalisation of unacceptable social practices causing bodily injury (such as female circumcision) and the acceptance of other practices, which also cause bodily harm or disfigurement (such as male circumcision and tattoos) which are tolerated.

Martina's situation

Martina may consider herself fortunate in having found Mr Walker, who is prepared to operate on her. Nowadays, it is very unlikely that any surgeon in this country would carry out this operation. Even private practice would not permit such an operation as the surgeons would risk being struck off the GMC register and if they are also NHS employees, lose their NHS employment. It may be that surgeons overseas would be prepared to carry out the operation.

Conclusion

Clearly, what is required is more research into body dysmorphic disorder and the developments of treatments to ameliorate or cure the condition. It may be that less drastic medical treatments, such as the temporary paralysis of the limb, may assist the sufferer. The danger is that unless such alternatives are found, in the absence of any law making these operations an exception to our criminal laws and standards of professional practice, patients such as Martina will end up on the railway line, possibly suffering much greater harm.

References

British Medical Association (2001) *Guidelines on Female Genital Mutilation*. BMA, London

Charter D, Kennedy D (2001) Doctors put on alert for girl butchery. *The Times* 21 August

Gillian H (2000) Surgeon happy he removed healthy limbs. *The Times* 1 February: 7

Law Commission (1995) *Consent in the Criminal Law*. No 139. HMSO, London

Royal College of Nursing (1998) *Position Paper 20. Female Genital Mutilation (Female Circumcision)*. RCN, London

R. v. *Brown* [1993] 2 All ER 75

23

Consent and the scope of professional practice

> **Box 23.1: Case scenario**
>
> Staff nurse Fawn was asked to take on the role of getting the patients to sign the consent forms before surgery was carried out. She was concerned at the legality of her being asked to undertake this since she would not be carrying out the operations. What is the law?

Introduction

In relation to consent, it should always be remembered that the signed consent form is not the consent, but evidence that consent has been given (*Chapter 3*). To be valid, the patient must be mentally competent and understand what invasion of his/her person is intended. Consent is, therefore, part of a process in which the patient is given the necessary information relating to the decisions which have to be made and then, without duress or fraud, the patient agrees that the proposed treatment can go ahead.

In addition, information must be given to the patient about any reasonably foreseeable risks of harm which could occur even if all care were taken. Failure to provide this information according to the reasonable professional standard (ie. the Bolam test) (*Bolam* v. *Friern Hospital Management Committee* [1957]) could, if harm were to occur to the patient, leave the trust open to an action for its vicarious liability for negligence by staff in failing to give the appropriate information to patients.

What should be taken into account in obtaining the consent?

It follows from the above that the person giving the information to the patient must understand what is proposed and must be able to explain to the patient, in words which he/she can understand, the nature of the proposed operation. Any additional procedures which may be necessary, and for which the patient's consent is required, would also have to be explained to the patient. If the person who is giving the information to the patient is not the same person who is to carry out the procedure, great care is necessary to ensure that the patient is not given any inaccurate information or any false assurances. For example, the patient may inquire if the operation is to be carried out by a consultant. If, in fact, it is a junior doctor who is to carry out the operation, it would clearly be wrong for the patient to be told that the consultant would be performing it.

Where the patient seeks additional information, the person discussing the treatment with the patient must be able to provide this information. If the questions cannot be answered, there must be a referral to the appropriate person before the form is signed so that the patient can have these questions answered fully and accurately.

The scope of professional practice

It is legally possible for nurses and other health professionals, such as physiotherapists or radiographers, to obtain consent for procedures which are to be carried out by doctors. This would be regarded as an expanded role activity. Therefore, all the principles which relate to *The Scope of Professional Practice* as laid down by the UKCC would apply (UKCC, 1992a). These principles are summarised in *Table 23.1*.

Table 23.1: Principles for adjusting *The Scope of Professional Practice* (UKCC, 1992a)

The registered nurse, midwife or health visitor:

1. Must be satisfied that each aspect of practice is directed to meeting the needs and serving the interests of the patient or client

2. Must endeavour always to achieve, maintain and develop knowledge, skill and competence to respond to those needs and interests

3. Must honestly acknowledge any limits of personal knowledge and skill and take steps to remedy any relevant deficits in order effectively and appropriately to meet the needs of patients and clients

4. Must ensure that any enlargement or adjustment of the scope of personal professional practice must be achieved without compromising or fragmenting existing aspects of professional practice and care and that requirements of the Council's *Code of professional conduct* (UKCC, 1992b) are satisfied throughout the whole area of practice

5. Must recognise and honour the direct or indirect personal accountability borne for all aspects of professional practice

6. Must, in serving the interests of patients and clients and the wider interests of society, avoid any inappropriate delegation to others which compromises those interests

The UKCC's scope document has been revoked by the publication of the new *Code of professional practice* of the Nursing and Midwifery Council (NMC). However, the principles set out in *Table 23.1* are still valid. The revised *Code of professional practice* was agreed by the UKCC and the shadow NMC (NMC, 2002) and published when the NMC came into being. It came into force in June 2002. Clause 6 requires the registered practitioner to maintain her professional knowledge and competence. Clause 6.2 states:

> *To practise competently, you must possess the knowledge, skills and abilities required for lawful, safe and effective practice without direct supervision. You must acknowledge*

> *the limits of your professional competence and only undertake practice and accept responsibilities for those activities in which you are competent.*

This clause could apply to all health professionals undertaking expanded role activities. The essential requirement is that the health professional must act within the scope of his/her competence. It would be wise to ensure, as in any other expanded role activity, that a procedure is drawn up specifying the level of competence required by the health professional, the actions which he/she should take in the event of certain questions being raised, and that all patients could, if they so wish, speak to a doctor.

The standard which the health professional must satisfy is the reasonable standard of care of the health professional who would usually undertake that role. It would be no defence for a physiotherapist to argue that the reason certain information was omitted, which would usually have been given to a patient, was because a physiotherapist, rather than a doctor, was carrying out that activity.

Training and competence of the health professional

Any expanded role activity requires appropriate training and supervised practice to be made available to the health professional. In the case of the expanded role of explaining procedures to the patient and communicating to the patient (so that the patient ultimately signs the consent form) the health professional should be sure that he/she has the necessary supervised practice, always admits ignorance and refers the patient to the doctor who is to carry out the procedure when necessary.

The Department of Health (DoH, 2001a) guidance on consent is given in *Box 23.2*.

Box 23.2: The Department of Health's guidance on consent (DoH, 2001a)

The clinician providing the treatment or investigation is responsible for ensuring that the patient has given valid consent before treatment begins, although the consultant responsible for the patient's care will remain ultimately responsible for the quality of the medical care provided.

The General Medical Council guidance states that the task of seeking consent may be delegated to another health professional, as long as that professional is suitably trained and qualified. In particular, they must have sufficient knowledge of the proposed investigation or treatment, and understand the risks involved, in order to be able to provide any information the patient may require. Inappropriate delegation (eg. where the clinician seeking consent has inadequate knowledge of the procedure) may mean that the 'consent' obtained is not valid. Clinicians are responsible for knowing the limits of their own competence and should seek the advice of appropriate colleagues when necessary.

Bristol Royal Infirmary inquiry into paediatric cardiac surgery (The Kennedy Report)

The report of the inquiry into paediatric cardiac surgery at the Bristol Royal Infirmary (DoH, 2001b) made clear recommendations about the process of consent (*Table 23.2*). (See also *Chapters 2, 4* and *5* where other recommendations are discussed.) The Bristol report also recommends that patients should be referred to information relating to the performance of the trust, of the specialty and of the consultant unit (a consultant and the team of doctors who work under his/her supervision).

Table 23.2: Recommendations in relation to consent from the report of the inquiry into paediatric cardiac surgery at Bristol Royal Infirmary (DoH, 2001b)

Recommendation 24:	The process of informing the patient, and obtaining consent to a course of treatment, should be regarded as a process and not a one-off event consisting of obtaining the patient's signature on a form
Recommendation 25:	The process of consent should apply not only to surgical procedures, but also to all clinical procedures and examinations which involve any form of touching. This must not mean more forms; it means communication
Recommendation 26:	As part of the process of obtaining consent, except when they have indicated otherwise, patients should be given sufficient information about what is to take place, the risks, uncertainties, possible negative consequences of the proposed treatment. Any alternatives, and the likely outcome to enable them to make a choice about how to proceed

The health professional, who takes on this expanded role of giving information to the patient and obtaining the patient's consent to the treatment proceeding, would also have to understand the performance figures and be able to explain the figures and their significance accurately to the patient.

Staff nurse Fawn's situation

It is clear from what has been said that to delegate to one staff nurse, ie. staff nurse Fawn in *Box 23.1*, the task of obtaining consent from patients for all the surgery which is to be undertaken is too vast a role for a nurse to take on competently and lawfully. However, it would be possible for staff nurse Fawn, after specific training, to discuss with patients who are having a specific type of surgery the details of that surgery, the associated risks and implications, answer the patients' questions and thereby obtain a valid consent. For staff nurse Fawn to take on an undefined responsibility over areas of treatment in which she has not had specific training would mean that she would not have the competence to undertake them safely. Further clarification is required of what staff nurse Fawn should undertake and the training and knowledge necessary for her to be competent.

Conclusion

As the professional role of the different health professionals expands, it is probable that obtaining the consent of the patient to proposed treatment and diagnostic procedures will increasingly become the responsibility of health professionals, other than the person carrying out the treatment. There are no legal barriers to prevent other health professionals undertaking this expanded role activity: there are no statutes which make it illegal for health professionals other than doctors to carry this activity out.

However, the common law rule that the health professional must satisfy the reasonable standard of care according to the Bolam Test does apply. It is the health professional's personal and professional responsibility to ensure that he/she is competent to undertake this activity and the onus is upon him/her to refuse to undertake it, if there are reasonable grounds for believing that he/she lacks the capacity.

References

Bolam v. *Friern Hospital Management Committee* [1957] 1 WLR 582

Department of Health (2001a) *Reference Guide to Consent for Examination or Treatment*. DoH, London

Department of Health (2001b) *Learning from Bristol: the Report of the Public Inquiry into Children's Heart Surgery at the Bristol Royal Infirmary 1984–1995*. Command Paper CM 5207. DoH, London

Nursing and Midwifery Council (2002) *Code of professional conduct*. NMC, London

United Kingdom Central Council for Nursing, Midwifery and Health Visiting (1992a) *The Scope of Professional Practice*. UKCC, London

United Kingdom Central Council for Nursing, Midwifery and Health Visiting (1992b) *Code of professional practice for the nurse, midwife and health visitor*. UKCC, London

24

Consent and fertility treatment

> **Box 24.1: Case scenario (*R. v. Human Fertilisation and Embryology Authority ex p. Blood* [1997] 2 WLR 806)**
>
> Diane Blood was refused permission by the Human Fertilisation and Embryology Authority (HFEA) to use the stored sperm from her dead husband on the grounds that the husband had not given written consent for this use as required by the 1990 Act.

Introduction

As can be seen from the previous chapters in this book, much of the law on consent derives from case law: common law principles laid down by the judges which relate in particular to the law on trespass to the person (*Chapter 3*) and the law of negligence (*Chapters 4* and *5*). The area of fertilisation is one where there is a clear statutory framework for obtaining consent from the patient and others and covering the information which must be made available. (Another area where consent provisions have been laid down by statute is in organ donation by a non-related donor, see *Chapter 14*.) The Human Fertilisation and Embryology Act 1990 provides the statutory context within which fertilisation and the use of embryos can take place. The Human Fertilisation and Embryology Authority is responsible for issuing licences to approved centres which undertake work on fertilisation treatments under the provisions of the 1990 Act.

Consent provisions for retrieval, storage and use of human gametes under the Human Fertilisation and Embryology Act 1990

In the case scenario shown in *Box 24.1*, Diane Blood brought a case seeking judicial review of the Authority's refusal to license the infertility treatment. She and her husband who were married in 1991 decided to start a family at the end of 1994. Unfortunately, before she had conceived the husband contracted meningitis and she arranged for the sperm to be taken by electro-ejaculation from her husband as he lay in a coma. He died not long after. The Human Fertilisation and Embryology Authority refused to agree to allow her to have the necessary treatment using the sperm on the grounds that the statutory consent requirements had not been complied with. In addition, they refused to allow the export of the sperm so that the treatment could be carried out abroad. The Court of Appeal (*R. v. Human Fertilisation and Embryology Authority ex p. Blood* [1997] 2 WLR 806) held that as a result of the restrictions under Section 4(1)(b) and Schedule 3 the 1990 Act (see below) she could not have been lawfully treated with the sperm in this country. However, she would be permitted to receive treatment in Belgium according to Article 59 of the EC treaty. She subsequently became pregnant and gave birth. In 2002 it was reported that she had given birth to a second child, again conceived through use of the dead husband's sperm.

The statutory provisions

Section 4(1) of the Act states that:

> No person shall
>
> (a) store any gametes, or
>
> (b) in the course of providing treatment services for any woman, use the sperm of any man unless the services are being provided for the woman and the man together or use the eggs of any other woman.
>
> (c) mix gametes with live gametes of any animal,except in pursuance of a licence.

Under section 12 the general conditions of granting a licence require that there is compliance with the consent provisions set out in Schedule 3 (S.12(c)). Schedule 3 of the Human Fertilisation and Embryology Act is shown in *Box 24.2*.

Paragraphs 3–8 of Schedule 3 give further details on the consent requirements. Paragraph 3 on the procedure for giving consent is shown in *Box 24.3*.

Paragraph 5 of Schedule 3 prevents the receipt or use of a person's gametes for the treatment of others unless there is an effective consent by that person to their being so used and they are used in accordance with the terms of the consent. (This paragraph does not apply to the use of a person's gametes for the purpose of that person, or that person and another together, receiving treatment services. The Court of Appeal considered that this exception could not cover the situation of Diane Blood since the husband was dead and so the treatment services could not be described as for the use of 'that person and another together'). Paragraph 6 requires an effective consent to be given to the use of a person's gametes for the creation of any embryo *in vitro*. Paragraph 7 requires an effective consent to be given by a woman before an embryo is taken from her for any purpose. (This paragraph does not apply to the use of a woman's embryo for her own treatment purposes.)

Box 24.2: Schedule 3 Human Fertilisation and Embryology Act 1990 Consents to use of gametes or embryos

1. A consent under this Schedule must be given in writing and, in this Schedule, 'effective consent' means a consent under this Schedule which has not been withdrawn.

2. (1) A consent to the use of any embryo must specify one or more of the following purposes:

   (a) use in providing treatment services to the person giving consent or that person and another specified person together,

   (b) use in providing treatment services to persons not including the person giving consent, or

   (c) use for the purposes of any project of research,

   and many specify conditions subject to which the embryo may be so used.

2. A consent to the storage of any gametes or any embryo must:

   (a) specify the maximum period of storage (if less than the statutory storage period)

   and

   (b) state what is to be done with the gametes or embryo if the person who gave the consent dies or is unable because of incapacity to vary the terms of the consent or to revoke it,

   and may specify conditions subject to which the gametes or embryo may remain in storage.

3. A consent under this Schedule must provide for such other matters as the Authority may specify in directions

4. A consent under this Schedule may apply:

   (a) to the use or storage of a particular embryo, or

   (b) in the case of a person providing gametes, to the use or storage of any embryo whose creation may be brought about using those gametes,

   and in the paragraph (b) case the terms of the consent may be varied, or the consent may be withdrawn, in accordance with this Schedule either generally or in relation to a particular embryo or particular embryos.

Box 24.3: Paragraph 3 of Schedule 3 Procedure for giving consent

1. Before person gives consent under this Schedule:
(a) he must be given a suitable opportunity to receive proper counselling about the implications of taking the proposed steps, and
(b) he must be provided with such relevant information as is proper.

2. Before a person gives consent under this Schedule he must be informed of the effect of paragraph 4 (*Box 24.4*).

Box 24.4: Paragraph 4 of Schedule 3 Variation and withdrawal of consent

1. The terms of any consent under this Schedule may from time to time be varied, and the consent may be withdrawn, by notice given by the person who gave the consent to the person keeping the gametes or embryo to which the consent is relevant.

2. The terms of any consent to the use of any embryo cannot be varied, and such consent cannot be withdrawn, once the embryo had been used:
(a) in providing treatment services, or
(b) for the purposes of any project of research.

Paragraph 8 relating to the storage of gametes and embryos is shown in *Box 24.5*.

Box 24.5: Paragraph 8 of Schedule 3 Storage of gametes and embryos

1. A person's gametes must not be kept in storage unless there is an effective consent by that person to their storage and they are stored in accordance with the consent.

2. An embryo the creation of which was brought about in vitro must not be kept in storage unless there is an effective consent, by each person whose gametes were used to bring about the creation of an embryo, to the storage of the embryo and the embryo is stored in accordance with those contents.

3. An embryo taken from a woman must not be kept in storage unless there is an effective consent by her to its storage and it is stored in accordance with the consent.

Subsequent developments

Following the Diane Blood case, the Minister of Health appointed a committee under the Chairmanship of Professor Sheila McLean to review the consent provisions in the Human Fertilisation and Embryology Act 1990. A questionnaire was sent out for public consultation and the committee published its report in December 1998 (Department of Health, 1998). In general, it recommended that there should be no change in the common law. However, it was suggested that there could be an amendment to the requirements of written consent to storage so that HFEA had the discretion to waive the consent requirements in Schedule 3 of the 1990 Act for storage in the situation of an unconscious patient where it may be in the best interests of that person to remove and store gametes if treatment was likely to result in sterility on recovery. In August 2000, the Government published its response to the McLean report (Department of Health press announcement, 25 August 2000).

It accepted all the recommendations of the report and went further, suggesting a retrospective effect:

❖ The father's name should be allowed to appear on birth certificates where his sperm has been used after his death.

❖ The legal position on consent and removal of gametes should remain unchanged: gametes can be taken from an incapacitated person who is likely to recover, if the removal of gametes is in their best interests.

❖ The HFEA should have the power to permit the storage of gametes where consent has not been given, so long as the gametes have been lawfully removed. This will also benefit children who are about to undergo treatment which will affect their future fertility. (Legislation will be required to implement this.)

❖ Families will be able to make these birth certificate changes retrospectively.

❖ The best practice is for written consent to be obtained, since this most clearly constitutes effective consent. Where there is doubt over whether an effective consent has been obtained, this should be a matter for the courts.

The Government has not recommended that there should be any legislative change over permitting the export.

Centre for Reproductive Medicine v. *U* [2002]

Similar issues over the use of sperm posthumously arose in a recent case. A wife appealed against a high court decision which permitted the destruction by the reproductive centre of her late husband's sperm, which had been surgically removed and stored. Prior to the sperm being removed, the husband had signed a consent form in which he had agreed, *inter alia*, that the sperm could be used after his death. He later withdrew this aspect of his consent at the request of a specialist nursing sister. Both the centre and the nursing sister had ethical objections to the posthumous use of sperm. The wife contended that the husband had withdrawn his consent reluctantly and only because he believed that if he did not, the centre would cease or postpone fertility treatment. The Court of Appeal dismissed the wife's appeal. It held that the husband's withdrawal of consent to the posthumous storage and the use of his sperm had not been actuated by undue influence. Without an effective consent from the husband, the continued storage and later use of his sperm by the centre had been rendered unlawful by virtue of the Human Fertilisation and Embryology Act 1990.

Separated women and the right to use embryos

A further challenge to the provisions of the Human Fertilisation and Embryology Act 1990 started in September 2002 when two women sought to stop their former partners destroying their frozen fertilised embryos (Gibb, 2002). In the case of one woman, she had cancer and before the treatment started she placed six frozen embryos into storage. During treatment her ovaries were removed. Subsequently, she and her partner split up and the partner is refusing to give consent to the continued storage and use of the frozen embryos. The Act requires that both partners must give consent. The case is due to be heard in 2003.

Conclusions

This is an interesting area and the advantages of statutory regulation over the consent provisions are clearly in the interests of all those involved in fertility treatments, though as the Diane Blood case illustrated, there are grounds for a less restrictive framework. Issues concerning gametes are included in a Consultation Report issued by the Department of Health (DoH, 2002) *Human Bodies, Human Choices*. Views were invited on such issues as to: whether the HFEA should have the power to waive the requirement for personal consent to the storage of gametes for the duration of a child's incapacity and if so should parental or court consent be required; should courts have a power to consent to continued storage of gametes once someone reaches the age of eighteen; should the courts have the power to remove gametes from a mentally incapable adult and also be able to specify what should happen to the gametes in the event of a person's death or permanent incapacity? The consultation ended in October 2002 and at the time of writing it is anticipated that the next stage will be a White Paper or Bill.

This is an area of tight control over consent provisions and it may be that some of the lessons learnt from statutory provisions for consent in fertility treatments and also statutory provisions for consent in organ donation by live unrelated donors (*Chapter 14*) could pave the way to statutory provisions for consent to treatment.

References

Centre for Reproductive Medicine v. *U* [2002] EWCA Civ 565, The Independent May 1 2002 CA

Department of Health (1998) Sheila McLean Review of the Common Law Provisions Relating to the Removal of Gametes and of the Consent Provisions in the Human Fertilisation and Embryology Act 1990. DoH, London

Department of Health (2000) Press announcement. DoH, London: 25 August

Department of Health (2002) *Human Bodies, Human Choices: The law on human organs and tissue in England and Wales*. A consultation report. Department of Health and Wales National Assembly

Gibb F (2002) Separated women seek right to use frozen embryos. *The Times* 12 September

R. v. *Human Fertilisation and Embryology Authority ex p. Blood* [1997] 2 WLR 8 06 [1997] 2All ER 687

25

Consent and the mentally disordered

Introduction

In *Chapter 7* we considered the law relating to decision making on behalf of those adults who lacked the mental capacity to make their own decisions, and noted the power recognised at common law for decisions to be made in the best interests of such persons. In *Chapter 11* we discussed what was meant by the term 'best interests'. In this chapter we look at the present statutory provision relating to mentally disordered adults and consider briefly legislative changes which are anticipated within the next year. The introduction of the European Convention of Human Rights into the laws of the UK has resulted in many cases being brought by the mentally disordered with significant results.

Long-term detained patients

Under the provision of Part IV of the Mental Health Act 1983 those patients who are detained under long-term detention provisions (eg. Sections 2, 3, 37 and 41) can, in certain circumstances, be given compulsory treatment. For these patients the Act covers all possible treatments for mental disorder, both in emergency and non-emergency situations. The provisions are set out in *Box 25.1*.

> **Box 25.1: Provisions under Part IV of the Mental Health Act 1983 on consent to treatment (Sections 57, 58 and 63)**
>
> 1. Treatments involving brain surgery or hormonal implants can only be given with the patient's consent which must be certified and only after independent certification of the consent and of the fact that the treatment should proceed (Section 57).
> 2. Treatments involving electroconvulsive therapy, or medication where three months or more have elapsed since medication was first given during that period of detention can only be given either (a) with the consent of the patient and it is certified by the patient's own registered medical practitioner or another registered medical practitioner appointed specifically for that purpose that he is capable of understanding its nature, purpose and likely effects, or (b) the registered medical practitioner appointed specifically certifies that the patient has refused or is incapable of consenting but agrees that the treatment should proceed (Section 58).
> 3. All other treatments: these can be given without the consent of the patient provided they are for mental disorder and are given by or under the direction of the responsible medical officer (Section 63).

In 2002, a Broadmoor patient challenged the fact that he was given treatment under Section 58 and sought leave to seek judicial review of his treatment, which had been prescribed by his responsible medical officer (RMO) and supported by a second opinion appointed doctor (SOAD). The patient had expert opinion from an independent doctor that the treatment was not appropriate. The Court of Appeal (*R. v. Broadmoor Hospital*) held that the court would have to consider the medical necessity of the proposed treatment and the capacity of the patient and, any future forcible treatment in the light of the Articles of the European Convention and the three doctors should be called to give evidence. The Court of Appeal also held that Article 6 of the

Convention required that the certification process by the second opinion appointed doctor should involve the making of an independent and primary judgement on the desirability and propriety of treatment and should not comprise merely a review of the responsible medical officer's decision.

Urgent treatment for longer term detained patients

In an emergency or where the patient has withdrawn his consent to treatment under section 58, the provisions of section 57 and 58 do not apply, and Section 62 applies. Section 62 is shown in *Box 25.2.*

Box 25.2: Section 62 Mental Health Act 1983

Any treatment which is immediately necessary to save the patients life.

Treatment which is not irreversible if it is immediately necessary to prevent serious deterioration.

Treatment which is not irreversible or hazardous if it is immediately necessary to alleviate serious suffering.

Treatment which is not irreversible or hazardous if it is immediately necessary and represents the minimum interference necessary to prevent the patient from behaving violently or being a danger to himself or others.

Section 62 enables different treatments to be given according to the degree of urgency and whether they are irreversible or hazardous. *Box 25.2* illustrates the provisions.

Irreversible is defined as, 'if it has unfavourable irreversible physical or psychological consequences'; and hazardous is defined as, 'if it entails significant physical hazard'.

Section 63 treatments

It can be seen from *Box 25.1* that those treatments which do not come under 57 or 58 come under section 63 and can be given without the consent of the patient provided that the treatment is for mental disorder and is given by or under the direction of the responsible medical officer. In the case of *B.* v. *Croydon HA* [1995] the Court of Appeal held that treatment for mental disorder could include treatment to relieve the symptoms of the mental disorder as well as treatment ancillary to the core treatment. It could therefore cover compulsory feeding of a patient suffering from anorexia. (Force-feeding of anorexia patients was also permitted under Section 63 in two other cases: *Riverside Mental Health NHS Trust* v. *Fox* [1994] and *Re KB.* (1994).) The definition of treatment for mental disorder was given an extended meaning in the case of *Tameside and Glossop Acute Services Trust* v. *CH*, where the court held that a patient detained under the Mental Health Act could be given a Caesarean section as treatment for her mental disorder (see *Chapter 12*). In the light of the decision of the Court of Appeal in St George's NHS Trust (1998), where a woman suffering from mental disorder is detained under the Mental Health Act 1983 and is refusing a Caesarean, best practice would ensure that an application were made to court for a determination of her capacity and (if it is held that she lacks mental capacity) a determination of what is in her best interests.

Patients not detained under the Mental Health Act

In the case of *R.* v. *Bournewood Community and Mental Health NHS Trust*, the House of Lords held that patients who did not have the capacity to consent to admission to psychiatric hospital could be detained under common law powers. Concerns about a possible clash between this principle and Article 5 of the European Convention of Human Rights are to be taken account of in the new legislation to replace the Mental Health Act 1983, and the White Paper reforming the Mental Health Act recommends safeguards for those who are not detained under the Act, but do not have the mental capacity to agree to admission or treatment.

Future mental health legislation: Reform of the Mental Health Act

An expert committee was set up by the Government in 1998 under the chairmanship of Professor Richardson to review the Mental Health Act 1983. Its terms of reference included the degree to which the current legislation needed updating to ensure that there is a proper balance between safety (both of individuals and the wider community) and the rights of individual patients. It was required to advise the Government on how mental health legislation should be shaped to reflect contemporary patterns of care and treatment and to support its policy as set out in the paper, *Modernising Mental Health Services* (DoH, 1998). The Expert Committee presented its preliminary proposals which set out the principles on which any future legislation should be based in April 1999 and its full report was published in November 1999. The Government presented its proposals for reform in 1999 with a final date for response by 31 March, 2000 (DoH, 1999b)

The proposals include the reasons for proposed changes and cover the following topics:

- guiding principles for a new Mental Health Act
- processes of applying compulsory powers
- criteria for compulsory care and treatment
- the new tribunal's remit
- discharge and aftercare

- interface with the criminal justice system
- treatment
- safeguards.

The guiding principles which the Consultation paper suggests should be contained in a new Mental Health Act are set out in *Box 25.3*.

Box 25.3: Guiding principles to be included in a new Mental Health Act

❖ Informal care and treatment should always be considered before recourse to compulsory powers.

❖ Patients should be involved as far as possible in the process of developing and reviewing their own care and treatment plans.

❖ The safety of both the individual patient and the public are of key importance in determining the question of whether compulsory powers should be imposed.

❖ Where compulsory powers are used, care and treatment should be located in the least restrictive setting consistent with the patient's best interests and safety and the safety of the public.

Other principles, recommended by the Review Committee and which the Government considers should be included in a Code of Practice on the new Act are shown below:

- non-discrimination
- patient autonomy
- consensual care
- reciprocity
- respect for diversity
- equality
- respect for carers
- effective communication
- provision of information

- evidence-based practice
- processes of applying compulsory powers.

This is not the place to consider changes to the definition of mental disorder or proposals on the detention of patients. As far as changes in the statutory provisions for compulsory treatment are concerned, the Committee suggested that the common law powers to act out of necessity would continue to provide authority to detain and treat. In relation to the statutory treatment provisions, the Committee recommended that special safeguards should apply to electro-convulsive therapy, polypharmacy and feeding contrary to the will of the patient. Statutory safeguards for the protection of the patient would include:

- The Mental Health Act Commission
- hospital managers
- a nominated person (instead of the nearest relative)
- advocacy
- carers.

Other proposals related to long-term patients who lack mental capacity and who are at present outside the protection of the Mental Health Act 1983 (*R*. v *Bournewood Community and Mental Health NHS Trust*). It is proposed that there should be a new statutory framework provided for them as recommended in the Lord Chancellor's proposals (Lord Chancellor, 1999).

Draft Mental Health Bill and consultation paper

The Department of Health published a White Paper in December 2000 setting out its proposals for reform. Unusually, a draft mental health bill was published in 2002 prior to its introduction into Parliament for debate, together with a consultation document and explanatory notes.

(Normally, following a White Paper, the next anticipated stage would have been a Bill introduced into Parliament.)

Consultation ended in September 2002 and at the time of writing the results of this consultation exercise are unknown. It is appearing increasingly unlikely that legislation will be enacted and implemented before 2004.

The Draft Bill Part 2 contains provisions for care plans (Clause 26) to be prepared for the patient by the clinical supervisor and contain information to be prescribed by regulations. The clinical supervisor must consult, if practicable, the patient's nominated person and any carer of the patient about the medical treatment to be specified in the plan. The Bill requires that there is independent scrutiny and authorisation by the Mental Health Tribunal for the use of compulsory powers beyond the initial twenty-eight-day period. An application has to be made to the Tribunal for an order authorising the medical treatment of the patient. Clause 31 sets out all the information which has to be put before the tribunal when this authorisation is sought. Clauses 33–35 and 38–39 cover the application and authorisation of further orders. Clause 38(7) covers the power of the Tribunal to order that the patient is to be provided with medical treatment as a non-resident, by making himself available for treatment during specified times. Part 4 of the Bill covers medical treatments to which special safeguards apply (such as any surgical operation for destroying brain tissue) and also special provisions for compulsory treatments including electroconvulsive therapy and other treatments to be specified in regulations. Part 5 covers the case of informal patients who are not capable of consenting. Clause 121 requires a clinical supervisor, if satisfied that the patient is incapable of consenting to treatment and would either resist treatment or is at risk of suicide or causing serious harm to others, to ensure that the treatment must be authorised under Part 2 of the Bill. Specific safeguards are laid down to protect compliant incapacitated patients receiving treatment in NHS or independent hospitals. It must be emphasised that all these clauses are in draft and we must await the completion of the Parliamentary stages and Royal Assent before the Bill becomes an Act. There may then be some time before the Act is actually brought into force.

Conclusions

The task of framing the new Mental Health legislation is an exacting one. The new laws must walk the tightrope between the protection of the rights of the individual, and in particular article 5 of the European Convention of Human Rights (*Appendix*) and the protection of the public. Unless this balance is achieved, there are likely to be a considerable number of challenges to the courts of the UK and the European Court of Human Rights in Strasbourg.

References

B. v. *Croydon HA* [1995] 1 All ER 683

Department of Health (1998) *Modernising Mental Health Services*. DoH, London

Department of Health (1999) *Review of the Mental Health Act 1983: Report of Expert Committee* November 1999. DoH, London

Department of Health (1999b) *Reform of the Mental Health Act 1983 — Proposals for Consultation*. Cm 4480. Stationery Office, London

Department of Health (2000) White Paper Reforming the Mental Health Act. Cm 5016. DoH, London

Department of Health (2002) Draft Mental Health Bill. Cm 5538–1; Explanatory notes (Cm 5538–11) and a consultation document (Cm 5338–111). DoH, London

Re KB. (adult) (mental patient: medical treatment) (1994) 19 BMLR144

Law Commission (1995) *Mental Incapacity*. Report No 231. The Stationery Office, London

Lord Chancellor (1999) *Making decisions on behalf of mentally incapacitated adults*. Stationery Office, London

Riverside Mental Health NHS Trust v. *Fox* [1994] 1 FLR 6614

R. v. *Bournewood Community and Mental Health NHS Trust Ex p L* [1999] 1 AC 458

R. v. *Broadmoor Hospital (and others)* [2002] Lloyd's reports Medical 41

St George's Healthcare NHS Trust v. *S*; *R* v. *Collins ex parte S* (1998) 44 BMLR 160 CA; [1998] 3 All ER 673

Tameside and Glossop Acute Services Trust v. *CH* (A patient) [1996] 1 FLR 762

26

Overview

This final chapter, attempts, in the light of the relevant statutes, the common law and the Department of Health guidance, to draw out the main principles which have been explored in this book.

Consent as part of a process

The first point to emphasise is that consent is not simply a signature on a form: it is the outcome from a process of communication between clinician and patient over the nature of the treatment and investigations proposed and the risks and benefits which could occur. Communication should be a two-way process and the questions of the patient should be answered fully and honestly. The signature should be evidence that this process has been followed and that the patient consents. Consent can also be evidenced by word of mouth and by non-verbal communication, but in situations where there are risks, it is preferable to obtain the patient's signature.

Distinction between trespass to the person and breach of the duty of care to inform

— broad consent

If the patient understands what is proposed and gives consent to that invasion of his/her person, then the patient would not be successful in an action for trespass to the person (assault or battery). A trespass to the person is a civil wrong — one of a group known as 'torts' — and is actionable without the person proving that harm has been suffered. In contrast, failure to inform the patient of the significant risks of substantial harm arising would give rise to an action in negligence for breach of the duty to inform the patient according to the reasonable standard of care (ie. the Bolam test; *Bolam* v. *Friern Hospital Management Committee* [1957]). In this latter action, harm must have occurred.

Competence

In order to give a valid consent a person must have the mental capacity to understand the information which is being given to him/her. There is a presumption in favour of capacity, but this can be displaced if evidence suggests a lack of capacity. In the case of Re MB., the Court of Appeal held that a person lacks the mental capacity to make a decision if:

a)   the patient is unable to comprehend and retain the information which is material to the decision, especially as the the likely consequences of having or not having the treatment in question.

b)   the patient is unable to use the information and weigh it in the balance as part of the process of arriving at the decision (see *page 98*).

Voluntary and without fraud

The consent must also be given with the free will of the mentally competent adult and without any deception. The Department of Health guidance warns of the dangers of patients being pressurised by parents or family members as well as health or care professionals. Care should be taken to avoid coercion which invalidates consent, especially where the patient is under involuntary detention as in prison or a mental hospital (DoH, 2001, paragraph 3 and 3.1).

Withdrawal of consent

Consent can usually (there are exceptions under the Human Fertilisation and Embryology Act 1990 [*Chapter 24*]) be withdrawn at any time, but checks should be made to ensure that the patient has the capacity to withdraw the consent. For example, a patient may as a result of pain or panic ask for the treatment to stop. In a situation where the patient, having given a valid consent, objects during the process of treatment and asks for the practitioner to stop, the Department of Health suggests that it is good practice for the practitioner to establish the patient's concerns and explain the consequences of not completing the procedure (DoH, 2001, paragraphs 18 and 18.1).

Advance refusals (living wills)

Advance refusals are valid at common law (ie. judge-made, case law), if at the time they were made the patient was mentally competent, the refusal was witnessed and the contents apply to the situation which has arisen and at this later time the patient lacks capacity.

Adults lacking mental capacity

If mental incapacity has been established, healthcare professionals have a duty to act in the best interests of the patient following the Bolam Test (*Re F. (mental patient: sterilisation)* [1990]). Legislation providing for decision making on behalf of a mentally incapacitated adult is awaited, although a White Paper has been published (Lord Chancellor, 1999). If there is doubt over the validity of a living will, an application can be made to the court and the patient kept alive until the court has decided on its validity. Professionals withholding care on the basis of a valid living will would be acting lawfully. The Court of Appeal has issued guidelines on the action which should be taken if a person is refusing necessary care and treatment and there are reasonable doubts over the person's mental capacity to refuse (*Re MB. (an adult: medical treatment)* 1997).

Children and young persons

A young person of sixteen and seventeen years has a statutory right to give consent to treatment which includes medical, surgical and dental treatment, anaesthetic and diagnostic procedures (Family Law Reform Act 1969 — section 8(1) and (2)). Parents of children below eighteen years also have the right to give consent to treatment on the child provided it is in the best interests of the child. Children and young persons (ie. persons under eighteen years) do not have the right in law to refuse life-saving treatment, if that is in their best interests (*Re W. (a minor) (medical treatment)* [1992]). However, overruling a young person's refusal of treatment would not be lightly done. Children under sixteen years, while they do not have a statutory right to give consent, are able at common law to give a valid consent, provided that they have sufficient understanding and intelligence to enable them to understand fully what is involved in a proposed intervention (ie. they are considered to be Gillick-competent — *Gillick* v. *West Norfolk and Wisbech AHA* [1986]).

Withdrawing and withholding life-prolonging treatment

Table 26.1: Reasons for withdrawing and withholding life-saving treatment (including resuscitation)

- The patient refuses to have it and the patient is mentally competent

- The patient has drawn up a valid advance refusal which applies to the situation

- The treatment would not succeed

- The long-term prognosis of the patient is such that treatment is not in the best interests of a mentally incapacitated patient

Life-saving treatment (including resuscitation) can be withdrawn or withheld for the reasons cited in *Table 26.1*. These principles were confirmed by the House of Lords in the case involving the Hillsborough victim Tony Bland (*Airedale NHS Trust* v. *Bland* [1993]). The Department of Health has issued guidance on 'not for resuscitation' instructions (NHS Executive, 2000). It recommends the guidance issued by the British Medical Association (BMA), the Resuscitation Council (UK) and the Royal College of Nursing which was issued in 1999 and recently updated (BMA, Resuscitation Council (UK), RCN, 2001). Withholding life-saving treatment from patients in a persistent vegetative state has been held not to be contrary to Articles 2 or 3 of the European Convention on Human Rights (*NHS Trust A.* v. *Mrs M.* and *NHS Trust B.* v. *Mrs H. Family Division* [2001]).

Other situations

As this book has shown, there are many and varied situations where these basic principles have to be applied. Thus, the law relating to consent and research, organ donation, and Caesarean sections have all been considered in detail. Other situations, such as the law relating to those compulsorily detained under the Mental Health Act 1983 have not been explored in detail since the Government is at present proposing major changes to mental health legislation (DoH, 1999; DoH, 2002) (see *Chapter 25*).

Conclusions

Over the next few years there are likely to be further developments in the law relating to consent. In particular, legislation on decision making on behalf of the mentally incapacitated is awaited in England and Wales although Scotland already has its Adult Incapacity Act 2000. Replacing the common law with statutory provision should clarify many of the current uncertainties. For example, under the common law principle of acting in the best interests of a mentally incapacitated adult, how much compulsion, if any, could be used to ensure that a person who was refusing necessary treatment could be compelled to have it?

At present, the Department of Health has decided against any legislation for advance refusals considering that the common law covers the situation. However, as *Chapter 17* showed, this gives rise to many uncertainties.

It is the intention of the Department of Health to update its reference guide on a regular basis, so that any legal changes are included. This should be of considerable assistance to the registered practitioner on whom the personal and professional responsibility falls to ensure that the rights of the patient as set out in the Articles of the European Convention of Human Rights and in statute law and common law are always upheld.

References

Airedale NHS Trust v. *Bland* [1993] AC 789

Bolam v. *Friern Hospital Management Committee* [1957] 1 WLR 582

BMA, Resuscitation Council (UK), RCN (2001) *Decisions Relating to Cardiopulmonary Resuscitation: A Joint Statement from the BMA, Resuscitation Council (UK) and the RCN*. BMA, London

Department of Health (1999) *Reform of the Mental Health Act 1983*. The Stationery Office, London

Department of Health (2001) *Reference Guide to Consent for Examination or Treatment*. DoH, London

Department of Health (2002) *Draft Mental Health Bill*. Stationery Office, London

Gillick v. *West Norfolk and Wisbech AHA* [1986] AC 112

Lord Chancellor (1999) *Making Decisions on Behalf of Mentally Incapacitated Adults*. Lord Chancellor's Office, London

NHS Executive (2000) *Executive Resuscitation Policy*. HSC 2000/028. NHS Executive, Leeds

NHS Trust A. v. *Mrs M*. and *NHS Trust B*. v. *Mrs H. Family Division* [2001] Lloyd's Rep Med 27

Re C. (adult: refusal of medical treatment) [1994] 1 All ER 819

Re F. (mental patient: sterilisation) [1990] 2 AC 1

Re MB. (an adult: medical treatment) (1997) 38 BMLR 175; *St George's Healthcare NHS Trust* v. *S.* [1998] 3 All ER 673

Re W. (a minor) (medical treatment) [1992] 4 All ER 627

Further reading

Brazier M (1992) *Medicine, Patients and the Law.* Penguin Books, London

Card R (1998) *Cross and Jones' Criminal Law.* 14th edn. Butterworths, London

Denis IH (1999) *The Law of Evidence.* Sweet and Maxwell, London

Dimond BC (1999) *Patients' Rights, Responsibilities and the Nurse.* 2nd edn. Quay Books, Mark Allen Publishing Limited, Dinton, Salisbury

Dimond BC (1997) *Legal Aspects of Occupational Therapy.* Blackwell Scientific Publications, Oxford

Dimond BC (1996) *Legal Aspects of Child Health Care.* Mosby, London

Dimond BC (2002) *Legal Aspects of Confidentiality.* Quay Books, Mark Allen Publishing Limited, Dinton, Salisbury

Dimond BC (2002) *Legal Aspects of Pain Management.* Quay Books, Mark Allen Publishing Limited, Dinton, Salisbury

Dimond BC (2002) *Legal Aspects of Midwifery.* 2nd edn. Books for Midwives Press/Butterworth Heinemann, Oxford

Dimond BC, Barker F (1996) *Mental Health Law for Nurses.* Blackwell Science, Oxford

Dimond BC (1997) *Legal Aspects of Care in the Community.* Macmillan Press, London

Dimond BC (1998) *Legal Aspects of Complementary Therapy Practice.* Churchill Livingstone, Edinburgh

Dimond BC (2002) *Legal Aspects of Nursing.* 3rd edn. Pearson Education, Harlow

Dimond BC (1999) *Legal Aspects of Physiotherapy.* Blackwell Science, Oxford

Finch J, ed (1994) *Speller's Law Relating to Hospitals.* 7th edn. Butterworths, London

Hocton A (2002) *The Law of Consent to Medical Treatment.* Sweet and Maxwell, London

Hunt G, Wainwright P, eds (1994) *Expanding the Role of the Nurse.* Blackwell Scientific Publications, Oxford

Hurwitz B (1998) *Clinical Guidelines and the Law.* Radcliffe Medical Press, Oxford

Ingman T (1996) *The English Legal Process.* 6th edn. Blackstone Publishing, London

Jones R (2001) *Mental Health Law Manual.* 7th edn. Sweet and Maxwell, London

Kennedy I, Grubb A (2000) *Medical Law and Ethics.* Butterworth, London

Kennedy T (1998) *Learning European Law.* Sweet and Maxwell, London

Kloss D (2000) *Occupational Health Law.* 3rd edn. Blackwell Scientific Publications, Oxford

Knight B (1992) *Legal Aspects of Medical Practice.* 5th edn. Churchill Livingstone, Edinburgh

Markesinis BS, Deakin SF (1999) *Tort Law.* 4th edn. Clarendon Press, Oxford

McHale J, Fox M Murphy J (1997) *Health Care Law.* Sweet and Maxwell, London

McHale J, Tingle J (2001) *Law and Nursing.* 2nd edn. Butterworth Heinemann, Oxford

Montgomery J (1997) *Health Care Law.* Oxford University Press, Oxford

Pitt G (2000) *Employment Law.* 4th edn. Sweet and Maxwell, London

Reeves M, Orford J (2002) *Fundamental Aspects of Legal, Ethical and Professional Issues in Nursing.* Quay Books, Mark Allen Publishing Limited, Dinton, Salisbury

Rowson R (1990) *An Introduction to Ethics for Nurses.* Scutari Press, London

Rumbold G (1999) *Ethics in Nursing Practice.* 3rd edn. Baillière Tindall, London

Skegg PDG (1998) *Law, Ethics and Medicine.* 2nd edn. Oxford University Press, Oxford

Stone J, Matthews J (1996) *Complementary Medicine and the Law.* Oxford University Press, Oxford

Tingle J, Cribb A, eds (1995) *Nursing Law and Ethics.* Blackwell Science, Oxford

Tschudin V, Marks-Maran, D (1993) *Ethics: A primer for nurses.* Baillière Tindall, London

White R, Carr P, Lowe N (1989) *A Guide to the Children Act.* Butterworth, London

Young AP (1989) *Legal Problems in Nursing Practice.* Harper and Rowe

Young AP (1994) *Law and Professional Conduct in Nursing.* 2nd edn. Scutari Press, London

Zander M (1995) *Police and Criminal Evidence Act.* 3rd edn. Sweet and Maxwell, London

Glossary

Accusatorial	A system of court proceedings where the two sides contest the issues (contrast with inquisitorial).
Act	Of Parliament, statute.
Actionable *per se*	A court action where the claimant does not have to show loss, damage or harm to obtain compensation, eg. an action for trespass to the person.
Actus reus	The essential element of a crime which must be proved to secure a conviction, as opposed to the mental state of the accused (*mens rea*).
Adversarial	The approach adopted in an accusatorial system.
Advocate	A person who pleads for another: it could be paid and professional, such as a barrister or solicitor, or it could be a lay advocate either paid or unpaid.
Assault	A threat of unlawful contact (trespass to the person).
Balance of probabilities	The standard of proof in civil proceedings.
Barrister	A lawyer qualified to take a case in court.
Battery	An unlawful touching (see trespass to the person).
Bolam Test	The test laid down by Judge McNair in the case of *Bolam* v. *Friern HMC* on standard of care expected of a professional in cases of alleged negligence.
Burden of proof	The duty of a party to litigation to establish the facts, or in criminal proceedings the duty of the prosecution to establish both the *actus reus* and the *mens rea*.
Cause of action	The facts that entitle a person to use.
Civil action	Proceedings brought in the civil courts.
Civil wrong	An act or omission which can be pursued in the civil courts by the person who has suffered the wrong (see torts).
Committal proceedings	Hearing before the magistrates to decide if a person should be sent for trial in the crown court.

Common law Law derived from the decisions of judges, case law, judge-made law.

Conditional fee system A system whereby client and lawyer can agree that payment of fees is dependent upon the outcome of the court action.

Coroner A person appointed to hold an inquiry (inquest) into a death in unexpected or unusual circumstances.

Criminal wrong An act or omission which can be pursued in the criminal courts.

Damages A sum of money awarded by a court as compensation for a tort or breach of contract.

Declaration A ruling by the court, setting out the legal situation.

Dissenting judgement A judge who disagrees with the decision of the majority of judges.

Distinguished (of cases) The rules of precedent require judges to follow decisions of judges in previous cases, where these are binding upon them. However, in some circumstances it is possible to come to a different decision because the facts of the earlier case are not comparable to the case now being heard, and therefore the earlier decision can be 'distinguished'.

Ex gratia As a matter of favour, eg. without admission of liability, of payment offered to a claimant.

Expert witness Evidence given by a person whose general opinion, based on training or experience, is relevant to some of the issues in dispute.

Re F. ruling A professional who acts in the best interests of an incompetent person who is incapable of giving consent, does not act unlawfully if he follows the accepted standard of care according to the Bolam Test.

Hierarchy The recognised status of courts which results in lower courts following the decisions of higher courts (see precedent). Thus, decisions of the House of Lords must be followed by all lower courts unless they can be distinguished (see above).

Indictment A written accusation against a person, charging him with a serious crime, triable by jury.

Injunction	An order of the court restraining a person.
Inquisitorial	A system of justice whereby the truth is revealed by an inquiry into the facts conducted by the judge, eg. Coroner's court.
Judicial review	An application to the High Court for a judicial or administrative decision to be reviewed and an appropriate order made, eg. declaration.
Litigation	Civil proceedings.
Magistrate	A person (Justice of the Peace or stipendiary magistrate) who hears summary (minor) offences or indictable offences which can be heard in the magistrates court.
Mens rea	The mental element in a crime (contrasted with *actus reus*).
Ombudsman	A commissioner (eg. health, local government) appointed by the Government to hear complaints.
Plaintiff	Term formerly used to describe one who brings an action in the civil courts. Now the term claimant is used.
Practice direction	Guidance issued by the head of the court to which they relate on the procedure to be followed.
Precedent	A decision which may have to be followed in a subsequent court hearing (see hierarchy).
Prima facie	At first sight, or sufficient evidence brought by one party to require the other party to provide a defence.
Privilege	In relation to evidence, being able to refuse to disclose it to the court.
Proof	Evidence which secures the establishment of a claimant's or prosecution's or defendant's case
Prosecution	The pursuing of criminal offences in court.
Quantum	The amount of compensation or the monetary value of a claim.
Reasonable doubt	To secure a conviction in criminal proceedings the prosecution must establish beyond reasonable doubt the guilt of the accused.
Solicitor	A lawyer who is qualified on the register held by the Law Society.
Statute law (statutory)	Law made by Acts of Parliament.

Strict liability	Liability for a criminal act where the mental element does not have to be proved; in civil proceedings liability without establishing negligence.
Subpoena	An order of the court requiring a person to appear as a witness (*subpoena ad testificandum*) or to bring records/documents (*subpoena duces tecum*).
Summary offence	A lesser offence which can only be heard by magistrates.
Tort	A civil wrong excluding breach of contract. It includes: negligence, trespass (to the person, goods or land), nuisance, breach of statutory duty and defamation.
Trespass to the person	A wrongful direct interference with another person. Harm does not have to be proved.
Ultra vires	Outside the powers given by law (eg. of a statutory body or company).
Vicarious liability	The liability of an employer for the wrongful acts of an employee committed while in the course of employment.

List of abbreviations

BMA	British Medical Association
CHI	Commission for Health Improvement
CNST	Clinical Negligence Scheme for Trusts
CPR	Cardiopulmonary resuscitation
DoH	Department of Health
DHSS	Department of Health and Social Services
DNR	Do not resuscitate
HFEA	Human Fertilisation and Embryology Authority
LREC	Local Research Ethics Committee
NFR	Not for resuscitation
NICE	National Institute for Clinical Excellence
NMC	Nursing and Midwifery Council
MREC	Multicentre research ethics committee
PVS	Persistent vegetative state
RCN	Royal College of Nursing
RCPCH	Royal College of Paediatric and Child Health
RMO	Responsible medical officer
SOAD	Second opinion appointed doctor
UKCC	United Kingdom Central Council for Nursing, Midwifery and Health Visiting
ULTRA	Unrelated live transplant regulatory authority

Appendix: Schedule 1 to the Human Rights Act 1998

Article 2 Right to Life

1. Everyone's right to life shall be protected by law. No one shall be deprived of his life intentionally save in the execution of a sentence of a court following his conviction of a crime for which this penalty is provided by law.

2. Deprivation of life shall not be regarded as inflicted in contravention of this Article when it results from the use of force which is no more than absolutely necessary:

    (a) in defence of any person from unlawful violence;

    (b) in order to effect a lawful arrest or to prevent the escape of a person lawfully detained;

    (c) in action lawfully taken for the purpose of quelling a riot or insurrection.

Article 3 Prohibition of torture

No one shall be subjected to torture or to inhuman or degrading treatment or punishment.

Article 4 Prohibition of slavery and forced labour

1. No one shall be held in slavery or servitude.

2. No one shall be required to perform forced or compulsory labour.

3. For the purpose of this Article the term 'forced or compulsory labour' shall not include:

    (a) any work required to be done in the ordinary course of detention imposed according to the provisions of Article 5 of this Convention or during conditional release from such detention;

    (b) any service of a military character or, in case of conscientious objectors in countries where they are recognised, service exacted instead of compulsory military service;

    (c) any service exacted in case of an emergency or calamity threatening the life or well-being of the community;

    (d) any work or service which forms part of normal civic obligations.

Article 5 Right to liberty and security

1. Everyone has the right to liberty and security of person. No one shall be deprived of his liberty save in the following cases and in accordance with a procedure prescribed by law:

    (a) the lawful detention of a person after conviction by a competent court;

    (b) the lawful arrest or detention of a person for non-compliance with the lawful order of a court or in order to secure the fulfilment of any obligation prescribed by law;

(c) the lawful arrest or detention of a person effected for the purpose of bringing him before the competent legal authority on reasonable suspicion of having committed an offence or when it is reasonably considered necessary to prevent his committing an offence or fleeing after having done so;

(d) the detention of a minor by lawful order for the purpose of educational supervision or his lawful detention of the purpose of bringing him before the competent legal authority;

(e) the lawful detention of persons for the prevention of the spreading of infectious diseases, of persons of unsound mind, alcoholics or drug addicts or vagrants;

(f) the lawful arrest or detention of a person to prevent his effecting an unauthorised entry into the country or of a person against whom action is being taken with a view to deportation or extradition.

2. Everyone who is arrested shall be informed promptly, in a language which he understands, of the reasons for his arrest and of any charge against him.

3. Everyone arrested or detained in accordance with the provisions of paragraph 1(c) of this Article shall be brought promptly before a judge or other officer authorised by law to exercise judicial power and shall be entitled to trial within a reasonable time or to release pending trial. Release may be conditioned by guarantees to appear for trial.

4. Everyone who is deprived of his liberty by arrest or detention shall be entitled to take proceedings by which the lawfulness of his detention shall be decided speedily by a court and his release ordered if the detention is not lawful.

5. Everyone who has been the victim of arrest or detention in contravention of the provisions of this Article shall have an enforceable right to compensation.

Article 6 Right to a fair trial

1. In the determination of his civil rights and obligations or of any criminal charge against him, everyone is entitled to a fair and public hearing within a reasonable time by an independent and impartial tribunal established by law. Judgement shall be pronounced publicly but the press and public may be excluded from all or part of the trial in the interests of morals, public order or national security in a democratic society, where the interests of juveniles or the protection of the private life of the parties so require, or to the extent strictly necessary in the opinion of the court in special circumstances where publicity would prejudice the interests of justice.

2. Everyone charged with a criminal offence shall be presumed innocent until proved guilty according to law.

3. Everyone charged with a criminal offence has the following minimum rights:

(a) to be informed promptly, in a language which he understands and in detail, of the nature and cause of the accusation against him;

(b) to have adequate time and facilities for the preparation of his defence;

(c) to defend himself in person or through legal assistance of his own choosing or, if he has not sufficient means to pay for legal assistance, to be given it free when the interests of justice so require;

(d) to examine or have examined witnesses against him and to obtain the attendance and examination of witnesses on his behalf under the same conditions as witnesses against him;

(e) to have the free assistance of an interpreter if he cannot understand or speak the language used in court.

Article 7 No punishment without law

1.   No one shall be held guilty of any criminal offence on account of any act or omission which did not constitute a criminal offence under national or international law at the time when it was committed. Nor shall a heavier penalty be imposed than the one that was applicable at the time the criminal offence was committed.

2.   This Article shall not prejudice the trial and punishment of any person for any act or omission which, at the time when it was committed, was criminal according to the general principles of law recognised by civilised nations.

Article 8 Right to respect for private and family life

1.   Everyone has the right to respect for his private and family life, his home and his correspondence.

2.   There shall be no interference by a public authority with the exercise of this right except such as is in accordance with the law and is necessary in a democratic society in the interests of national security, public safety or the economic well-being of the country, for the prevention of disorder or crime, for the protection of health or morals, or for the protection of the rights and freedoms of others.

Article 9 Freedom of thought, conscience and religion

1.   Everyone has the right to freedom of thought, conscience and religion; this right includes freedom to change his religion or belief and freedom, either alone or in community with others and in public or private, to manifest his religion or belief, in worship, teaching, practice and observance.

2.   Freedom to manifest one's religion or beliefs shall be subject only to such limitations as are prescribed by law and are necessary in a democratic society in the interests of public safety, for the protection of public order, health or morals, or for the protection of the rights and freedoms of others.

Article 10 Freedom of expression

1.   Everyone has the right to freedom of expression. This right shall include freedom to hold opinions and to receive and impart information and ideas without interference by public authority and regardless of frontiers. This Article shall not prevent States from requiring the licensing of broadcasting, television or cinema enterprises.

2.   The exercise of these freedoms, since it carries with it duties and responsibilities, may be subject to such formalities, conditions, restrictions or penalties as are prescribed by law and are necessary in a democratic society, in the interests of national security, territorial integrity or public safety, for the prevention of disorder or crime, for the protection of health or morals, for the protection of reputation or rights of others, for preventing the disclosure of information received in confidence, or for maintaining the authority and impartiality of the judiciary.

Article 11 Freedom of assembly and association

1.   Everyone has the right to freedom of peaceful assembly and to freedom of association with others, including the right to form and to join trade unions for the protection of his interests.

2.   No restrictions shall be placed on the exercise of these rights other than such as are prescribed by law and are necessary in a democratic society in the interests of national security or public safety, for the prevention of disorder or crime, for the protection of health or morals or for the protection of the rights and freedoms of others. This Article shall not prevent the imposition of lawful restrictions on the exercise of these rights by members of the armed forces, of the police or of the administration of the State.

Article 12 Right to marry

Men and women of marriageable age have the right to marry and to found a family, according to the national laws governing the exercise of this right.

Article 14 Prohibition of discrimination

The enjoyment of the rights and freedoms set forth in this Convention shall be secured without discrimination on any ground such as sex, race, colour, language, religion, political or other opinion, national or social origin, association with a national minority, property, birth or other status.

Article 16 Restrictions on political activity of aliens

Nothing in Articles 10, 11 and 14 shall be regarded as preventing the High Contracting Parties from imposing restrictions on the political activity of aliens.

Article 17 Prohibition of abuse of rights

Nothing in this Convention may be interpreted as implying for any State, group or person any right to engage in any activity or perform any act aimed at the destruction of any of the rights and freedoms set forth herein or at their limitation to a greater extent than is provided for in the Convention.

Article 18 Limitation on use of restrictions on rights

The restrictions permitted under this Convention to the said rights and freedoms shall not be applied for any purpose other than those for which they have been prescribed.

The first protocol

Article 1

Every natural or legal person is entitled to the peaceful enjoyment of his possessions. No one shall be deprived of his possessions except in the public interest and subject to the conditions provided for by law and by the general principles of international law.
The preceeding provisions shall not, however, in any way impair the right of a State to enforce such laws as it deems necessary to control the use of property in accordance with the general interest or to secure the payment of taxes or other contributions or penalties.

Article 2

No person shall be denied the right to education. In the exercise of any functions which it assumes in relation to education and to teaching, the State shall respect the right of parents to ensure such education and teaching in conformity with their own religious and philosophical convictions.

Article 3

The High Contracting Parties undertake to hold free elections at reasonable intervals by secret ballot, under conditions which will ensure the free expression of the opinion of the people in the choice of the legislature.

Index of cases

Index of statutes

Index